knitting for good!

knitting *for* good!

A Guide to Creating Personal, Social & Political Change, Stitch by Stitch

BETSY GREER

TRUMPETER
Boston & London · 2008

TRUMPETER BOOKS
An imprint of Shambhala Publications, Inc.
Horticultural Hall
300 Massachusetts Avenue
Boston, Massachusetts 02115
www.shambhala.com

9 8 7 6 5 4 3 2

Printed in Canada

♾ This edition is printed on acid-free paper that meets the American National
Standards Institute Z39.48 Standard.

♻ This book was printed on 100% postconsumer recycled paper. For more
information please visit us at www.shambhala.com.

Distributed in the United States by Random House, Inc.,
and in Canada by Random House of Canada Ltd

A portion of the author's proceeds will be donated to Rwanda Knits, a nonprofit
corporation that helps create economically sustainable knitting cooperatives
for Rwandan and refugee women living in Rwanda. Learn more about them at
www.rwandaknits.org.

Designed by Daniel Urban

Library of Congress Cataloging-in-Publication Data
Greer, Betsy.
Knitting for good: a guide to creating personal, social, and political change,
stitch by stich/Betsy Greer.—1st ed.
p.   cm.
Includes bibliographical references and index.
ISBN 978-1-59030-589-8 (pbk.: alk. paper)
1. Knitting. 2. Knitting—Miscellanea. I. Title.
TT820.G828 2008
746.43'2041—dc22
2008017179

Your hobby may be pie-baking, playing the piano, or potbelly-stove collecting, and you can sympathize with my enthusiasm, having an obsession of your own. Will you forgive my single-mindedness and my tendency to see knitting in everything?

—Elizabeth Zimmerman, *Knitting without Tears*

----

contents

acknowledgments

FIRST AND FOREMOST, MANY THANKS TO MY EDITOR, JENNIFER BROWN, FOR HER EAGLE EYE AND ENTHUSIASM. THANKS ALSO TO KAREN STEIB FOR HER KEEN COPYEDITING SKILLS AND JOY Gosney for her wonderful illustrations. Many thanks to Judith Shangold's knitting expertise as she looked over the patterns included in this book. To all the pattern and sidebar contributors and people who allowed me to interview them: I am so grateful for all of your hard work and wise words.

Second of all, thanks to everyone, friends and family alike, who listened and helped and kept me supplied with conversation that had nothing to do with craft when all I could think about was knitting! Thank you for the long walks, short runs, yoga in the living room, pep talks, cups of coffee, cupcakes, bad reality TV, pints of beer, glasses of wine, drives in the country, and late-night, long-distance phone calls. And most of all, thank you for your support and kind words over the past year—they have meant the world to me, and then some.

introduction

WALK INTO ANY KNITTING SHOP, AND CHANCES ARE THE
FIRST THING YOU'LL NOTICE IS ALL THE DIFFERENT TYPES OF YARN.
SUDDENLY YOU FIND YOURSELF IMMERSED IN A VAST SEA OF COLOR
and texture and endless possibilities, with each needle and skein ready to abet
you on whatever journey you may dream up. When I first started knitting, I
was ecstatic to learn how to create something wearable, armed only with two
sticks and some string. Watching yarn slowly turn into a scarf, hat, or sweater
awed me. And this was the first thing that really struck me about knitting—I
could make whatever I wanted in any color of my choosing. It was a possibility as ultimately liberating as it was initially daunting.

While my mind envisioned a wardrobe full of cabled sweaters and hand-
knit hoodies, as a new knitter, I was a bit concerned about the seemingly
incredibly repetitive nature of the craft. Only two stitches (knit and purl) ma-
nipulated in various ways continuously? For long periods of time? For fun?
By far there was a definite time when the end product seemed much more
desirable than the act of creativity that preceded it. How could repetitive
motions that created something at a snail's pace really capture my heart and
mind for long enough to finish a scarf (much less anything bigger) in today's
world of instant everything?

Thankfully, this concern, while understandable, was fleeting. When I was
finally comfortable enough with knitting that I no longer had to concentrate
on every movement my fingers made, I discovered that after completing a
few rows, the chatter in my mind dulled to a whisper. As I was used to a mind
filled with lengthy to-do lists and things to remember, this newfound respite
took some getting used to. While I had been a fledgling practitioner of yoga
and meditation for years, I was gob-smacked by the way knitting—even more
than meditation—connected me to that inner rhythm I had been trying so
hard to find. There was something about the way they both allowed me to

bring myself into the present, to just hang out and get comfortable (instead of trying to relive the past or jump ahead to the future) that was absolutely brilliant. Not surprisingly, soon after knitting helped me get acquainted with an inner stillness, I found myself better able to practice meditation, and once I found that rhythm, I was golden.

In time, knitting became more than just a simple way to pass the time or create my own garments. It calmed me, it connected me, it inspired me. It soothed me with the repetitive movements that also symbolized the growth of a garment or an accessory, each stitch simultaneously a push forward and a mark of time. Eventually, as I sought out knitting groups and took to knitting in public, this activity allowed me to talk to a whole host of people I never would have met otherwise. Thanks to the common denominator of knitting, I was able to connect with individuals who were older, younger, richer, not-so-rich, foreign, and local—all of us coming together through our love of craft.

As I became more proficient—and when I had given practically everyone I knew some sort of hand-knit item—I began looking for others, both near and far, who might benefit from my craft skills. During this quest, I realized that as I walked around town and watched the news, I was constantly bombarded by images of both humans and animals in need all over the planet, and it began to sink in that there were things I could do to help others just by knitting. I started with knitting scarves and hats for local homeless and domestic abuse shelters; the thought of bringing warmth and comfort to people with something soft and tangible seemed natural. The idea that my scarves were keeping people in my own community cozy allowed me to start processing how charity and compassion truly start in the smallest of actions. For far too many years, I got lost in the notion that to help the common good, you had to do big things or write big checks, but then again, that's what happens when you don't take the time to see how you as an individual are best equipped to aid others. While some people are meant to donate large sums of money, others are meant to donate their time, knowledge, or skills.

As time progressed, I kept expanding my focus toward the global scale, which for the most part is incredibly daunting and terrifyingly large. Every night on the news the world's problems seemed so vast that the thought of making a couple of hats for someone in need seemed laughable at best. But then I began to think about the traits that make handmade items unique—for example, how scarves knitted with hope and love always seem cozier on cold, lonely nights. While I wasn't volunteering to go live in a sub-Saharan refugee camp, I was doing *something*. Small? Yes. But desperately needed and treasured by the people receiving the scarves or hats or blankets. It was for those people, the ones who truly needed something that my hands could create in a few spare hours, that I started donating handmade items on an international level as well as a local one.

I think each of us is drawn to different ways to help; whether it's a charity across the world or down the street, the causes themselves often have an uncanny way of finding us. The first cause I chose to knit for was one that drew me in on a personal level, even though there is an endless list of organizations and charities and agencies that need help. Being something of a news junkie, I closely follow the whys and wheres and whens of the conflicts in Iraq and Afghanistan. When I started learning about the economic conditions in Afghanistan several years ago, I realized I couldn't *not* do something for the children there. After hearing about the war-torn history of the country, how few resources many of the people had, and how many Afghans had never experienced life without violent conflict, I felt especially inspired to help. This was a few years after the start of a well-known organization called Afghans for Afghans, a humanitarian project I had read about on various craft websites and message boards. When I learned about the societal conditions and the harsh winters in Afghanistan, I went through my yarn stash and quickly whipped up a few children's hats. It took little more than a couple of hours, and I made sure to use bright colors in the hope that they might bring a little bit of light to those who had endured a lifetime of strife.

Some people donate money to causes. Some help raise awareness for them via campaigning. I choose to knit. I know that what I create with my own hands will directly help someone in need by providing warmth. I can watch the garments grow on the needles in my hands, then send them off to an organization in the knowledge that they'll be distributed to people who can use them immediately. I like that.

There is always something incredibly humbling about packing up several teeny-tiny vests and a handful of hats in an equally tiny box and knowing that there are teeny-tiny children out there who would go cold without them.

About This Book

This is a book about expanding your relationship with craft so that it can become more a part of your everyday life, your personality, and your beliefs. Since my love of knitting grew from personal changes to later encompass community and global perspectives, that is how this book is organized. It is also my belief that when we make a change within ourselves and then apply it to our world, we can become better examples for others via our actions. Although this book is ultimately best read in chronological order, it is also written as a guide to help you jump-start your relationship with knitting (or sewing or basketball or what have you) however you need it, whether that is on a personal or global scale or somewhere in between.

Part 1 is about the personal effects of knitting and how you can benefit from just the simple act of knitting. One of the things I most often hear from new knitters (despite age or location) is, "I can't believe how relaxing knitting is!" This fortunate revelation is perhaps the first step toward making a more personal connection to your creativity. Through additional practice and a bit more concentration, there are many ways to benefit personally from knitting. This first section takes you from creating a view of craft that best suits you personally through to embracing the positive benefits that the process of knitting can provide.

Part 2 deals with ways you can aid your immediate community through craft and creativity. While knitting gifts for people you love is wonderful, knitting for others in your community can be just as, if not more, rewarding. Different communities have different needs, depending on location, culture, and economics, but every community has a want or need that can be met via creativity—you just may need to do a bit of brainstorming to see how your skills can be of use. This section is a starting point for connecting with family, friends, and others in your community.

The last part opens the view up to a global perspective and how our individual actions can affect the lives of others thousands of miles away. One of the remarkable things about knitting and handcrafts is their ability to transcend societal differences, as every culture has its own craft history based on its own idiosyncrasies. The widespread use of creative craft highlights the fact that although it is of great use when your community is without strife, you can still let your stitches do the talking even when people can't speak up or reach others. This section explores using craft to express emotion, make statements, and engage in activism.

This book is about taking your craft and creativity in hand and running with the possibilities. You will find sidebars throughout the chapters that have been written by some of my favorite people, those who inspire me to no end. Their kind words of wisdom and willingness to share their stories of creativity are what push me to dream bigger and expand my own definition of what it truly means to "be creative." At the end of each chapter, there is a knitting pattern contributed by a different talented knitter. All of the items within have either been donated to a charity of the knitter's choice or the proceeds from the sale of the pattern are going to charity. Each item and pattern represents part of the range of articles that can be donated to various charitable organizations. Each chapter also ends with an action, in case you would like to push your craft further and engage your creativity in new directions.

Finally, although this book centers on knitting, it speaks to all things handmade and creatively driven. Even though I identify most strongly with knitting, it is just one of the many crafts you can practice to make a difference personally, locally, and globally. The key is to find and explore a creative outlet—and to find a way to use the skills and knowledge you learn and hone to create positive change in the world. Don't worry about how big an improvement your action brings about; just create what you desire and set it free.

And while there are hundreds, if not thousands, of choices and paths before you, there are just as many personal stories and insights on how to use knitting for the good of ourselves and others. Just as the projects I may dream of as I step into a shop full of yarn may be worlds away from the creations you concoct, my experiences with knitting may be very different from yours.

My story is just one of many that could have been told, and I hope you keep that in mind as you read these pages and mold the ideas in them to fit your own life. Even though the specifics of our lives may be different, I believe that at our core, our experiences are more alike than we sometimes think. This book is written with those core similarities in mind; as no matter how we differ, we can all hold creativity in high esteem and value the lessons that knitting has to teach. This book is based on the belief that every time you pick up your knitting needles you have the opportunity to create positive change in the world.

It is my hope that what you read will make you think, create, and remember to take time to knit. I believe that if we take good care of ourselves, we can give more to others. Thank you for sharing this time with me. True magic happens when we create with our hands and dream from our hearts.

part one knitting for yourself

----

chapter one

reclaiming craft

I USED TO THINK THAT I DIDN'T FIND KNITTING; IT FOUND ME. HOW ELSE COULD I EXPLAIN HOW THIS GRANDMOTHERLY CRAFT MADE ITS WAY INTO MY FEMINIST, ACTIVIST LIFESTYLE? WHEN I first picked up the needles in 2000, knitters were still very much in the closet. I was embarrassed by my secret hobby, yet there was something about it that was irresistible. I found it relaxing, creative, and empowering, just as I find activism empowering. When I stop and think about how this craft came to me, I realize that there was a clear path that brought me to this point in my life—now a knitter of eight years. Understanding how I became a knitter let me relax deeper into my craft and reclaim the stereotypes so that I could truly be empowered by my choice to knit.

When you think of knitting, perhaps you also think of how it allows you to relax, create, and clothe. But how exactly did you find craft? Or did it find you, perhaps by chance? What led you to knit despite all the other crafty options? When we explore our craft roots, we can connect more deeply with what drives our creativity and compels us to make something. We can empower ourselves and our crafts by both embracing the domestic heritage of our work and becoming more fully aware of how we personally benefit from knitting. This chapter is about how finding and embracing the handmade can be an extremely personal and rewarding journey.

Letting Craft In

Like many people, I spent a somewhat extended part of my life trying to figure out just where I belonged. I tried things like skateboarding, playing music, starting a zine, hiking, and many other pursuits that resulted in either a bruised ego or bruised knees. For a long time, I honestly had no real idea where I fit in. I jostled between cliques and activities in the hope that one of them would fit me like a glove, allowing me the security and comfort to fully express myself.

When I discovered Riot Grrrl at the onset of the 1990s, it felt like what I had been waiting for my entire life. Here was a movement made up of women around the country (and later the world) who were unapologetic and unafraid to talk loudly and openly about their life experiences; this movement gave many of us the confidence and strength to speak out instead of staying silent. By using music and zines as modes of connection, Riot Grrrl managed to channel angst, energy, and modern politics in such a way that I felt for the first time that I could truly breathe deep—at last I knew I wasn't alone in wanting to fight instead of withering against injustice.

Listening to 7" records up in my room, I realized that many of the bands didn't have perfect production, pitch, or even timing. I would crank up my record player and dance and sing along to the lyrics, completely exhilarated to discover that there were people like me. I was beginning to understand that it was okay to be angry and unsure and politically and socially aware, and I was finally discovering that I didn't have to be perfect in order to do something. It was acceptable to not be good, because after all, I was learning, right? The notion that I could do something and screw it up without apology was novel and liberating. Being given the okay to get messy and dive into the learning process was what I needed to hear all those years ago, and it has stuck with me fiercely ever since.

This new way of thinking gave me the go-ahead to try a host of different things that I actually wanted to do instead of just doing the things my friends wanted me to do. It was my indoctrination into the world of the do-it-yourself (DIY) ideology and activism. By using my own creative drive as a positive force instead of allowing the wheels of consumerism to direct me, everything I did became part of my activism. Instead of pitting myself against others, I began to comprehend that if I wanted to make a magazine, I could write it and publish it myself; if I wanted to start a record company, I could start one in my bedroom. I finally felt completely free to explore my own creativity and identity.

I wish I could say my first yarn store experience was soon after I started knitting, but it took me months to finish my first project (a scarf made with yarn and needles that were given to me), and it was ages before I actually ventured into a shop that had more than just acrylic yarn. It was a small local store in Durham, North Carolina, that sold handmade jewelry and bags in the front and yarn in the back. I had decided to make scarves for my friends that I would call "Lucky Thirteens" as they were thirteen stitches across on size 13 needles. I wanted to make them out of mohair, so a yarn-buying trip was necessary.

I had little idea what I wanted; I simply needed mohair in the most vibrant colors I could find. Once I had made it past all the adorable handmade items in the front half of the shop, I found a whole wall of yarn in more colors than I had ever imagined. In minutes, I had felt dozens of skeins, not sure whether to take in the colors or the softness first. Having all those choices left me a bit shocked that I truly had free range to make whatever *I* wanted.

It was clear then, as I stood grinning at all those yarns, that knitting was for me. There was something incredibly enticing and intensely personal about the skeins upon skeins hung, stuffed, and stacked all over the back wall. There was something alluring about the needles and the projects that the women sitting at the round wooden table in the center of the store were working on and wearing. I found myself simultaneously intrigued and confused by the busyness of it all. There were colors from the entire rainbow surrounding me, from the perkiest of pinks to the boldest of blues, all filling cubbies built into the wall. Hung throughout the back of the store were various premade examples illustrating myriad ways to manipulate yarn. There were scarves, sweaters, and shawls, created with yarn available in the store, and hung up for inspiration. I won't go so far as to say that I underwent some sort of inner transformation that day, but I will say that I was completely shocked to see the vast range of possibilities—from the different textures and widths of yarn to the different items I could produce.

After touching and pawing a fraction of the various yarns before me, I was hit with the reality that it was tactile stimulation I had been missing. So often we are told not to touch, that when I was given this freedom, it felt a bit strange. Something in my heart warmed instantly and was inspired by the idea that I could turn something so seemingly simple as yarn into a creation of my own design. While I had always been fine creating with paper and pen or on a piano, neither of these activities felt so lovely and soft beneath my fingertips. As I circled the store touching one skein after another, it felt almost sinful to get my hands on so many different items that weren't made of metal or plastic.

When I look back on how I became a knitter, I see that the lessons I learned from Riot Grrrl have allowed me to fully embrace craft now. Theorist and writer Amy Lou Spencer echoed my thoughts in an e-mail: "The renewed interest in craft does stem from Riot Grrrl. Many of the people involved are those same people involved in the Riot Grrrl movement of the nineties. It is exciting that as we have grown older we are carrying the same ideals, a sense of independence and optimism, and are reinventing these to suit our lives." In other words, I'm not alone in wanting to be able to literally "craft my life," instead of letting it craft me.

While Riot Grrrl opened my eyes enough to try new things and explore my creativity, it also rooted me even deeper in my feminist views. For a time I considered anything even vaguely resembling the domestic arts to be completely disconnected from my creative path. But I found that in learning to knit, I would be discovering not only a way to create something I desired, but I would also have the opportunity to learn more about the daily experience of the millions of women who had taken up their needles before me. Knitting didn't make me a traitor to feminism; instead, I found myself able to connect with women of previous generations in a whole new way and celebrate their accomplishments. Although I wasn't in a club doing a microphone check or chaining myself to a building in protest, I was on the cusp of understanding what the power of positive activism could do, as well as the personal and communal benefits that came with it.

Cathy de la Cruz

CATHY DE LA CRUZ IS A FILMMAKER CURRENTLY LIVING IN SAN DIEGO, CALIFORNIA. ALONG WITH ERIN DONOVAN, SHE HOSTS A WEEKLY PODCAST ABOUT FILM AT SHOWMEYOURTITLES.BLOGSPOT.COM.

It's amazing that a political movement I believed in with all my heart when I was fourteen years old is still informing my life today at age twenty-seven. The Riot Grrrl movement of the 1990s helped me approach life with a DIY attitude and aesthetic. I believed I could make things and try things, from writing a fanzine to playing music in a band to all sorts of other things that girls weren't typically encouraged to do. I used to make zines in which I collaged and juxtaposed images and text together, and today I find myself using the same kinds of methods to create meaning and messages through my filmmaking, working as a DJ, and podcasting. I cohost a feminist film review podcast on the weekends and really believe a podcast today is what a zine was in the nineties—it's the kind of DIY communication that has been a big part of my life since Riot Grrrl, which deeply informed my views on art and politics.

Today, I stitch together my films, my DJ sets, and my podcast film critiques very much the way I stitched together fanzines and mix tapes when Riot Grrrl was in full bloom. Without Riot Grrrl, I might not have believed in myself enough to make art or be the feminist artist/filmmaker/DJ/teacher/writer/critic I am today. Even my career is stitched together like a zine, but I wouldn't have it any other way. Riot Grrrl provided so many women with the empowerment to make their own destinies.

I am so glad that as the Riot Grrrl movement floated away from mainstream press, the feminist-craft movement came to the fore. Anything that women enjoy always has to be designated a hobby and not a real form of art or political movement. Craft is just as important as any other art form, and I am so glad feminists have helped reclaim it. Just because we enjoy doing something, it doesn't mean we don't take it seriously or aren't really good at it.

Reclaiming Craft from Domesticity

I had to rethink my feminist views when I became attracted to knitting, and many others in the indie craft movement have had to do the same. Given the pervading stereotypes associated with knitting, it's no wonder that some of us were surprised to find we actually liked it—even loved it. Before 2000, the mere mention of the term *knitting* evoked many thoughts of grandmothers, domesticity, and other pastoral and seemingly nonradical things. Now, thanks to the recent craft resurgence, crafts such as knitting are being embraced and reclaimed by a new generation; we have the power to redefine *handmade* and all the baggage that may come with it. Crafts have been culturally redefined in a way that better reflects current views of feminism and domesticity.

But how did knitting get such an old-fashioned image? Although it has a long history dating back thousands of years, our most recent cultural perception of the craft was formed in the seventies, when women largely rejected traditional domestic arts in an attempt to gain social and economic equality. While some artists and crafters still created bodies of work from the late sixties through the early eighties, greater numbers of women started to move from the kitchen to the cubicle in order to prove that they were valuable entities in the corporate world as well as in the home. Starting with World War II, there had been a gradual increase in the number of women in the workforce; as men went to fight, women were recruited to work in the factories. According to data from the U.S. Department of Labor's Bureau of Labor Statistics, one in three women worked outside the home in 1950. By 1990, three out of every five women had joined the workforce. And although the increase was relatively steady over the forty intervening years, the biggest surge came in the 1970s with the powerful force of second-wave feminism and protests fighting for equal pay and equal treatment.

At that time, radical changes were being made in what had previously been culturally defined as "woman's work." Traditionally, many women had devoted serious effort to careers as homemakers and required a knowledge of crafts such as knitting, crochet, embroidery, needlepoint, and sewing to get the job done right. These domestic skills were passed along from generation to generation so, like their predecessors, young girls would be equipped to care for families when they married or, if necessary, to help their mothers while still at home. In the latter part of the century, however, the passing of such skills declined due to both improving technology and the equality movement. For feminists in the seventies, separating themselves from the home as a place of work was part of moving forward. This also meant that long-held traditions became seen as passive and retrogressive, and they needed to take a backseat in the name of progress.

As more and more women moved out of the home and into the office, crafts normally done in the domestic sphere were left behind; skills like knitting and needlework were perceived as the activities of mild-mannered women of previous eras. As the struggle for gender equality continued, the term *homemaker* gained a more negative connotation. Even though women were still responsible for all the same household tasks as before after their official workday ended, working outside the home was seen as progressive. As women's roles began to shift from two (mother and homemaker) to three (working woman, mother, homemaker), there simply wasn't enough time—or, given modern conveniences, the need—to do everything.

When I discovered how long it takes to knit an adult-sized sweater, I was stunned that such work was commonly (and errantly) portrayed as easy. And I bet when it was getting cold and a family only had threadbare sweaters from the previous year, knitting seemed like anything but pastoral and relaxing. We can view our current continuance of knitting as something that keeps the creativity of our crafty relatives alive and thriving, because it not only allows us to better understand their lives (and society before machines ruled the earth), but also to honor "woman's work." Our reclamation of the handmade is proof that these craft skills are valuable, worthwhile, and something to be proud of.

 Cinnamon Cooper

CINNAMON COOPER IS A CRAFTER WHO LIVES IN CHICAGO, ILLINOIS. WHEN NOT MAKING AND SELLING PURSES ON HER WEBSITE, POISE.CC, SHE'S PLANNING THE NEXT DIY TRUNK SHOW (DIYTRUNKSHOW.COM).

When I was a child, my mother's most prized possession was the antique Singer sewing machine that had belonged to her grandmother. The leather belt attached to the treadle slipped a little, but I remember her showing me how it worked. I was enthralled by the gold paint and the moving pieces and the magic that happened with two pieces of thread and a needle.

Ten years later I was riding my skateboard, listening to heavy metal, and trying desperately to find my niche in a social circle. I told my mother I wanted some wildly patterned, knee-length shorts that I thought would look awesome with my canvas high-top tennis shoes covered in marker drawings. Her reply: "Those shorts are so simple, you could make them." So we headed to the fabric store and thus began our lessons on my mother's more modern Singer sewing machine.

As I sat threading the needle, I had a revelation. "My great-grandmother did this. My grandmother did this. My mother does this. I'm doing this. I'm a link. It's my responsibility to learn these 'women's things' and pass them on." I pulled out my mother's book on needlecrafts and decided to teach myself as many of them as I could. I would intersperse rocking out with knitting, and popping ollies with learning embroidery stitches. I slowly got better at everything I tried, and the more I learned, the easier it was to learn.

I don't skate anymore, I'm embarrassed by those shorts I once thought were cool, and I've graduated to teaching others to craft. But I still have the same desire to be the link between my ancestors and my successors. And thanks to the Internet, I've had the chance to not only create a small business selling handcrafted bags (where a portion of the purchase price is donated to a non-profit organization I want to support), but to meet other women (and a few men) who skateboarded by day and crafted quietly alone at night. Because of the online social networking possibilities, we no longer have to be alone.

I'm able to create a bag that supports organizations fighting for the reproductive rights of women and to meet other women who want to do something creative and encourage them to make their world a better place through their creativity and skills. And it's worked. My friend Amy Carlton and I decided to create a craft show in 2003. We'd never been in a show before, nor did we have people we could ask about running one, but we decided to go for it. There have been five shows now, and each one gets bigger and better, with more customers wanting to buy handmade goods, more crafters wanting to show their wares, and more people asking how they can get involved "next year." While we've learned a great deal in the last five years and each show runs more smoothly than the one before it, I think it's important to stress that we didn't know what we were doing. We had an idea, we had a desire, we got enough feedback from friends to be hopeful, and we just forged ahead.

I hear so many aspiring crafters say, "I could never (fill in the blank) like you can." But they haven't tried. It is possible to teach yourself to sew, knit, fuse glass, throw pottery, quilt, make jewelry, and much more. Sure it's easier if a skilled and patient expert sits down and tells you how to do every single step, but then you become a practicer of steps—not a creator or a crafter, just a producer. Everyone's so worried about making mistakes, but I think we need to be worried about not trying things instead. Mistakes can frequently be righted, or at least we can realize that they aren't going to end a life. Surgeons need to be confident the first time they walk into an operating room; the rest of us can learn as we go. After all, I'm sure my great-grandmother didn't know any experts to explain seaming techniques when she was living on an isolated farm in the back country of Oklahoma, nor did she have the Internet with pictures and animated tutorials. What she did have were a few yards of scratchy fabric and a picture from a Sears and Roebuck catalog. But she took the tools and skills she had access to and made the best items she could. I have more tools, I'm surrounded by people with skills, and I feel like I'd be letting down the woman who polished her gilded Singer sewing machine if I didn't make the best use of what I have. So far, I don't feel that I have.

Embracing a New Feminism

For the majority of us who learned to knit within the past few decades, our only previous exposure to handcrafts was through our grandmothers or great-grandmothers. While some lucky individuals were taught the love of craft by their mothers, given the politics of the time, those of us who grew up in the seventies and eighties are more likely to have learned how to shoot hoops than how to knit hats. Now that I know how to knit, I fully appreciate those who came before me and clothed their whole families each winter without fail.

This domestic reclamation can be celebrated with pride and heads held high. We now have the opportunity to do so much more with our knitting. We don't have to knit those sweaters for the winter with all of our essentials just a shopping mall away. As a direct result of years of hardworking women who proved themselves just as capable as men of earning wages, we now have the freedom to make money for ourselves and then knit a sweater out of expensive cashmere bought with our own paycheck. Thanks to the early feminists, we can now do it all ourselves if we so choose. Talk about DIY! When we don an apron and start to cook or take measurements for a garment, we can be empowered by the notion that we are self-sufficient and *choosing* this path instead of following society's expectations. That's the real crux of all of this—we have the choice to knit or not knit, to bake or not bake. And while that may seem oversimplified and a bit trite, it is thanks to all the hard work of the women who labored to obtain equal rights that we can choose to reenter our kitchens without feeling like we're bending to cultural stereotypes. Feminism has given us the strength to explore our options instead of being concerned about regressing or kowtowing to cultural standards.

I am proud to be part of the demographic that is honoring and taking back the domestic, instead of viewing it as an obsolete construct. I truly believe that a sizable part of the craft resurgence's swift rise can be attributed to the increase of interest in the handmade, which was set afire by so many women's hunger for the domestic. Now that we realize we have the freedom to do as we wish, and after (given our endless options) we decide what life path we want to take, we can feel free to openly embrace the domestic for the first time in decades. Now that it's "okay" to like spending time in the kitchen or learning how to knit, we can be increasingly proud of ourselves for knowing how to wield a drill *and* a pair of knitting needles.

The role knitting plays in our lives is now largely up to us, since we can allow feminism to mesh with needlework. By making the domestic a source of pride and strength, we have the opportunity to culturally redefine "woman's work" as an act of progress instead of regression. It's almost the reverse situation of when I was younger and started playing sports with the boys; I wore my bruises and skinned knees as badges of honor because I knew that sports weren't always coed. My reclamation of the domestic was earned, just as all the time I spent running bases with boys helped me know that I could steal home and that being female didn't mean being demure. I'm excited to think that if one day I have a daughter of my own, I can teach her how to shoot a free throw and make a skirt. I am freer with my creativity because I have the opportunity to look to both the past and the present for inspiration.

Keeping Tradition Alive

As we continue to take our craft into the twenty-first century and give it new meaning, perhaps our greatest contribution to knitting is perpetuating it as a craft tradition. Now we can pass this skill on to others, as we dovetail history with the future.

When we view knitting as a long tradition of woman's work, we can start to appreciate the wisdom it leaves behind. The influence of the women before us is probably most noticeable when we see the end of a legacy. In an essay from the amazingly radical anthology *Women and Craft*, Sue Scott writes of how, after her grandmother died, she began to realize what she had lost besides a loved one: "When I wanted to produce a particular effect in a piece of work, I knew that she would have understood what I wanted and known the answer, but I lost the opportunity to ask her. Slowly, as I began to pick up the threads of my knowledge, I began to realize the value of the craft traditions practiced by the women of my family." Even though our crafts may live longer than we do, we shouldn't underestimate what we have to pass down to others. Once we're no longer here, our crafts will live, connecting generations, but we need to make sure we leave our words behind as well.

I'm lucky to still have both my grandmothers around, and when I'm with the one who knits, I'm always surprised by her vast knowledge of the crafty techniques she learned more than fifty years ago. She still remembers the argyle sock pattern she learned in college, although she does have notes on the measurements of my grandfather's feet written in shorthand on a piece of stationery. She remembers knitting in line for college classes without patterns at the ready, whereas today it's rare to see anyone knitting much of anything without a pattern stashed nearby. Sometimes she'll talk about knitting entire vests and sweaters from memory, and I can't help but wonder what knowledge could have been kept in existence if I had asked her earlier about her craft skills instead of decades later. Then again, at least I have the opportunity to ask her now.

What happens when older generations pass quietly on? Will they take their crafty tips and tricks with them? It is our job to keep the skills they have taught us alive—and we can only do that when we actively engage with knitters of past generations.

Thanks to the current interest in all things craft-related, the knowledge is being kept alive instead of disappearing like so many things formerly passed on by oral tradition. The Internet has helped this practice thrive with a plethora of online craft groups, blogs, and shops. The online craft community is vibrant, and now questions posed to online forums and groups can be answered in minutes, allowing for the creation of dialogues and multiple suggestions of solutions. All of a sudden, instead of doing the castoff you always do, you can gain knowledge from other eras, as well as other continents. Instead of not being able to solve a problem, the Internet fosters the predicament of deciding which of numerous solutions we should try first.

Knitting for Good Actions

Perhaps your return to crafts and the domestic happened much like mine, inspiring your thoughts about what feminism really means and how creativity is viewed by society. Perhaps it happened in some other way. If you're reading this book, I'm sure you've had

YOUR OWN PERSONAL REALIZATION THAT LED YOU TO KNITTING OR MAYBE ANOTHER CRAFT. I CHALLENGE YOU TO TAKE A LOOK BACK AT YOUR OWN EXPERIENCES AND SEE WHERE, WHEN, WHY, AND HOW THINGS STARTED TO CLICK FOR YOU. WHILE IT MAY BE TOTALLY DIFFERENT FROM MY STORY, I HAVE NO DOUBT THAT IT WAS JUST AS WELCOME, JUST AS HEARTENING, AND JUST AS NEEDED.

| Retrace Your Steps |

How did you come (or return) to craft? What paths crossed in your life to bring you toward knitting and/or the handmade? Take a minute to see where those paths started, ended, and met—how life led you to pick up the needles. What would the you of ten years ago think about your interest in the handmade now?

| Family History |

How many people in your family or social circle learned to knit from a family member? How many learned to knit from someone else or a book? How old were they? Do any of their stories sound like your own? Were they completely different? Were they unexpected? Discovering how people you care for fell in love with activities that grabbed their interest and fueled their creativity can give you a great deal of insight into your own metamorphosis.

Li's Reversible Herringbone Rib Scarf

Designed by Li Boesen

When I first started knitting, I learned how to make scarves, so it only seemed appropriate to place a scarf pattern in the first chapter. Scarves are not only easy projects to make for charity, but they are also items that individuals of all ages and both genders can wear. They keep you cozy against the winter wind and wrapped up tight when you need a little extra comfort.

This project comes from Li Boesen. It's a nice reversible pattern; one side features diagonal ribs, and the other has a plain, wide-ribbed look.

| FINISHED MEASUREMENTS |

7" x 65" after blocking

| YARN |

Manos del Uruguay Wool Clàsica (100% wool; 138 yards/100 grams): 2 skeins #113 Wildflowers

| NEEDLES |

One pair straight needles size US 9 (5.5 mm)

Change needle size if necessary to obtain correct gauge.

| GAUGE |

20 sts and 24 rows = 4" (10 cm) in pattern stitch

| NOTES |

RT: K2tog but don't slip sts from needle; insert right needle between the sts just knitted tog, and knit the first st again, then slip both sts from needle together.

Always slip (sl) as to knit.

| SCARF |

CO 34 sts.

Row 1: Sl 1, k rem sts.

Row 2: Sl 1, p1, *[RT] 3 times, p2; rep from *.

Rows 3 and 5: Sl 1, k1, *p6, k2; rep from *.

Row 4: Sl 1, p1, *k1, [RT] twice, k1, p2; rep from *.

Rep rows 2–5 for desired length. K 1 row. Bind off knitwise.

Blocking is required to get the proper effect of the herringbone rib. To block, soak in warm water for 15 minutes. Wrap in towel to remove most of the water. Lay flat to dry and pin to the appropriate size.

deepening our connection to craft

creativity and personal expression

KNITTING IS AN ACT OF IMAGINATION. ALTHOUGH PATTERNS MAY TAKE AWAY FROM SOME OF THE CREATIVE GUESSWORK, THE KNITTER IS STILL LARGELY RESPONSIBLE FOR CONJURING UP A FINISHED project and choosing all of the elements—color, fiber, gauge, and so forth. In this way, knitting allows us to explore our creativity, and what is creativity but a true expression of personality? We can knit big, cozy sweaters to hide in; lacy shawls to twirl in; or bright socks to dance in. What we are drawn to knit is often not just a reflection of our personal aesthetic, but a little clue to our character. One of the most wonderful aspects of knitting is that it allows us to explore our likes and dislikes and eventually our authentic sense of self. Once we gain this self-awareness, we can generally find the inspiration and energy to make decisions about how we live our lives. This chapter explores the positive benefits of craft and the ways knitting can help us live more ethically, holistically, and freely.

The Art and Craft of Knitting

What does the word *craft* mean? Today it is evolving to embody many different forms and definitions. We go crafting. We get crafty. And we hang out with craftsters. The first time I mentioned to a coworker that I was going to "spend my weekend crafting," he looked at me quizzically. When I then said, "I'm going to work on some knitting and sewing," he seemed to get it, even though this made him ask if I was going to my grandmother's house.

Just as knitting is being reclaimed from the domestic, craft is also going through a revolution on a broader scale. For me, discovering this whole new world of traditional crafts, especially knitting, was a bit like being a child again—I kept finding myself wide-eyed and hungry to learn new techniques or tricks. There was always, and still is, more to learn and someone else to teach, which strengthened my own confidence in my practice. Knitting quickly opened a whole world of creative expression for me, which was made even more profound because it was something I had never experienced through art as an adult.

Ever since the topic was bandied about with cavalier and exclusionary zeal in my university classes, I've been intimidated by art. There always seemed to be arcane and unspoken rules about what made one splotch on a canvas a work of art and another merely a paint spill. To me, art has always been expressed as "the other," something outside of the everyday experience, and quite frankly, entirely alien to anything I thought I could ever learn to produce. Where were the mistakes, the mishaps? Where was the artistic equivalent of Riot Grrrl bands to remind me that it was okay to "just be okay"? Years of art history classes may have allowed me to learn about some of the most amazingly created works on the planet, but they left me feeling like an outsider when it came to the act of expression itself.

The fact that art is often seen this way inevitably leads a large portion of society to feel cut off from it. I think this is another factor for the significant growth of interest in craft: it's not art. It's not "the other." Craft is something you can toy and experiment with instead of worrying that you are striving toward a certain goal or are setting yourself up for failure. The expectations for craft have always been completely different than those for art. Art goes on the wall to be admired, whereas craft is meant to be used. Because of its utile nature, craft has been able to bloom outside the voyeuristic and critical world of art. It has expanded and grown because, essentially, if you need a teapot and make one, no one's going to critique that teapot as long as it brews a mean cup of tea. Craft grew from usefulness into creative endeavor, whereas art has largely remained purely creative expression.

Because craft has fewer preconceptions and a more fluid definition, there are no limits to what can be done with it; you can quite simply do whatever you want. The strength of craft lies in its ability to jump-start our creativity by having few rules about who is a practitioner and who isn't. "Craft has accessibility. It is defined by the maker, and for this reason it is approachable to many," says Faythe Levine, director of the documentary *Handmade Nation*.

"You get to make craft what you want it to be—your job, your hobby, your community, your outlet from work, your gateway into the highbrow gallery world—craft is as big or little as one person makes it."

Craft, given its utilitarian (as opposed to aesthetic) roots, invites a sense of play. Sometimes in learning to knit, there can be a sense of constriction due to the initial awkwardness of handling needles and yarn simultaneously. And because we're so used to following directions, we can sometimes find ourselves strangely overwhelmed and stifled when we're given the freedom to create whatever we want.

Breaking through this conceptual wall can aid us in developing our creativity, whether we call ourselves makers, crafters, or artists. The problem is in the linguistic stereotyping of the words, not the words themselves. It's not that I'm anti-art, I'm just against the way that art can bring a sense of alienation instead of providing a wide, blank canvas for expression. The point is to expand and tease out your creativity. If you are easy on yourself, you can find that cozy niche where your mind wanders and itches to create instead of being paralyzed by all the other creative paths you could be taking.

Sally Fort

SALLY FORT WORKS AS A FREELANCE CONSULTANT FOR ART, CRAFT, DESIGN, MUSEUM, AND GALLERY PROJECTS. SHE WRITES ABOUT CRAFT ON HER BLOG, TINKERINGTIMES.TYPEPAD.COM, AND LIVES IN MANCHESTER, ENGLAND.

Craft gives a person control—over their work, personal satisfaction, barriers, and commitments. I recently carried out some research and found that many people make [craft projects] in order to be able to control their work life and accommodate their priorities as they want, rather than how traditional work patterns dictate. I know of one woman who, because of illness, isn't able to commit to a "normal" full-time job, but she creates a prolific number of craftworks and is very successful at selling them. Making is an alternative that gives her what she needs—an income, a workplace that accommodates her needs, a flexible work pattern that suits her energy level and physical abilities, and so on.

I was lucky enough to have been brought up by parents whose motto was "Give it a go. If it doesn't work, we'll try something else." It never occurred to me that I couldn't or shouldn't do these things.

I believe that craft is a system of belief—it enables expression and personal fulfillment such as control over personal circumstances and the chance to build relationships by buying into the stories, time, skill, and passion that has gone into creating a single, unique piece of work. I want the things I own to embody human properties, to be part of life in some way. There is something about crafts that makes me wonder about their physical or technical properties and thus exercise my brain. But more than that, they make me feel connected to other people so that I can see some commonality between the maker and myself, be it a style or a similar set of reference points. At the same time, being part of a larger community of makers gives me a set of new perspectives. It's about being part of a community, but also being challenged. That's not something a trip down to the local shopping center can offer.

When people ask me what I do, I say that I wear two hats. First, I manage art projects. These are usually for galleries, museums, or education and art agencies of some kind. Second, I manage contemporary craft and design projects. I never tell them I'm a maker. It's not a conscious thing, but when I think about it, I see my role as a facilitator. I like to weave webs that enable other people to do what they do. My textiles work is therefore a much more personal project, but in a social context, it provides the same things—the chance to talk to and work with other people, to swap information and help find new opportunities. I like to solve problems.

Sometimes it's for groups, organizations, or networks; sometimes it's more of a technical approach to my own making. I can spend days or weeks thinking about the angle or shape a particular pattern needs to be, how to strengthen it, how to make a set of two-dimensional parts come together to create a three-dimensional shape in just the way I want it.

Personal Expression

So what do we do with all of this newfound creativity? My creative energy led me to start exploring my own form of personal expression. And because I was now armed with knitting needles, I began toying with my personal style. As a knitter, I could suddenly make my own fashion choices from the very beginning of the garment. I had never realized before that I could make my own clothes. It may sound silly, but over the years it had become ingrained in my head that when you needed new clothes, you went to the mall—not the fabric store or the yarn store or the craft store. Although it was overwhelming at first, this realization was also quite spectacular because it meant that I could knit or sew whatever I wanted in the color of my choice, and as an added bonus, there would be no label attached that read "Made in (one of an ever-growing list of economically challenged countries)." The making would be all my own.

As I'm not outrageously adventurous, it's not surprising that the first thing I knitted was a scarf. When I was finished, the end result was so forlorn looking and rife with mistakes that it's still never been worn in public. The point is that what really captured my attention for this first project was the color—kelly green. It was a vibrant, almost shocking shade that was brighter than any color I had ever seen on a store-bought item, and because the length and width and gauge were also of my choosing, each aspect of the scarf had required me to make decisions. Errors and all, it was all mine.

Soon after the kelly green scarf, more scarves and some hats came in quick succession. There was something about the way these pieces made me feel when I wore them. They added punch to my outfits, and that delighted me. I mixed colors and patterns that probably should never have been combined in a single garment, but I didn't care because I had decided what went where; if I wasn't pleased with the result of my efforts, I could rearrange, restart, or change things until I was.

I suppose that it was this utilitarian aspect of knitting that really inspired me. Not only was I making something, but I was making something that I could actually use. Being able to wear my creations and interact with them from conception to finished garment encouraged my creativity even more.

It was this creative tinkering with my wardrobe that led me to some unforeseen changes in my personal beliefs, which then led to my personal fashion revolts. While at first I just loved to wear my own garments—pieces that felt truly like "me"—I started to realize that I was tired of wearing clothes that someone else had designed and deemed acceptable. Although readymade garments are available nearly everywhere in most countries of the world and making clothes at home is no longer a necessary chore, the decision to make or buy our wardrobe rests firmly in our own hands. Most days it may be more convenient to buy needed items—for example, when you snag a hole in your tights. But when we have the opportunity to make our own garments, we can truly feel good not only about making an item that perfectly suits our personal style, but about making a conscious decision to become aware of our constant consuming. Instead of viewing my knitting as just a way to create more work for myself, I soon started to see making my own clothes as a way to take responsibility for my actions and acquisitions. I realized that I did have a choice in the products I bought and I could control what I was consuming.

I'm not advocating that we should make everything by hand. But with a little forethought, we can assemble a wardrobe that suits us and our tastes instead of being limited to a specific range of choices offered and selected by someone else. I must admit, though I might just be too sentimental, I honestly believe that a handmade sweater will always be warmer than one made in a factory. Not just because it was made with love, but because it was made with a specific person in mind, which means that the garment is probably going to fit much better than one of the handful of sizes available in the sweaters at the local mall. While I may not win any scientific arguments with this, there is something undeniably magical about putting on a handmade garment for the first time. I'm talking about something that fits you as if it were made for you—because it *was* made for you. When we know that one person, rather than a host of people and machines in a factory, has control of a garment's creation from start to finish, we can step outside of the fashion consumer world, if only for a moment, and into a much warmer and more authentic place.

Kate Bingaman-Burt

KATE BINGAMAN-BURT IS AN ASSISTANT PROFESSOR OF GRAPHIC DESIGN AT PORTLAND STATE UNIVERSITY. ON HER WEBSITE, OBSESSIVECONSUMPTION.COM, SHE EXPLORES OUR CULTURAL LOVE-HATE RELATIONSHIP WITH BUYING AND SPENDING. THROUGH DRAWINGS AND PRINTS, SHE HIGHLIGHTS OUR OFTEN CONFLICTING RELATIONSHIP WITH OUR FINANCES.

I insist that viewers of my work (either on my website or in a gallery) can see the handmade quality in my work—from the crooked stitches on my pillows and dresses to the shaky line quality of my drawings. In no way can any of my products be mistaken for those created by a machine.

Part of Obsessive Consumption [OC] is about making the mundane special. I am taking a mass-produced product (consumer goods) and personalizing it. The consumer is no longer faceless. It is a reaction to the machine of the mass-produced product, and hopefully the viewer gets satisfaction from the personal interaction.

My work does not operate on a traditional functional level, but more as an object of contemplation. OC products hopefully work on two levels—formal (colors, design, composition) and conceptual (consumers' commentaries, transparency of personal consumerism, thinking about their own consumerism through my consumerism).

The slowness of craft reveals a certain layer of truth. The maker is able to meditate and/or critically focus on the subject of what is being made. This is what I find so special about working this way.

The Value of the Needle

In our quest for getting the most out of our money, sometimes we forget why we're able to pay a pittance for something right off the rack. When I learned to knit, I started to gain an understanding of the work that went into making a garment. Those seams certainly don't stitch themselves. Now when I buy new clothes, I find myself wondering who is really behind the factory labels. Those that say "Made in Vietnam (or the Philippines or Bolivia or China or somewhere else)" were sewn into the garments somewhere far, far away from the big-name designers and their original ideas. What good is a cheap T-shirt when the person who made it may be struggling for basic necessities? How many shirts passed under his or her eye each day on one of many assembly lines in a clothing plant? Sometimes I wish I could find an end to this endless circle of questions, but I know that they all just mean there's more work to be done to try to make things right.

By whipping out my credit card and supporting companies with questionable ethical practices, I was helping support businesses that believe that individuals in poorer countries deserve less money for their time than we do. Having worked numerous minimum wage jobs over the course of my life, I know that this is nothing but an injustice to people who are just trying to get by. As knitters, we have the tools to help in a small way by making items for ourselves and our loved ones instead of buying them. By deciding to make and restructure as much of my wardrobe as I can, I am consciously choosing to not support the actions of corrupt companies; although it may seem like a small action, it means the world to me.

As time progresses, I'm discovering that the more I knit, the less I want to consume. If I knit myself a pair of socks, not only do I appreciate the value of those socks more, but I can also be sure they weren't produced in a sweatshop. Unfortunately, making something by hand isn't always an option. Creating a garment by hand takes planning, and when you need something today for a dinner party this evening, it just may not be possible to whip up that gorgeous shawl after work and before the event. The trick here is knowing when to make and when to purchase, and if you go with the latter option, making a conscious decision to spend your money with ethics (instead of just cost) in mind. The tiny choices that may seem inconsequential can, when aggregated, add up to a host of handmade goods and money spent on what's necessary instead of solely on what's wanted.

Just the fact that some items in your closet were created by two hands, not whirring metal things, makes them that much more unique and special. The overall lesson to be learned in looking at what it takes to make something (and what it takes to buy something) is that we have a choice about what we wear and how it's made. This ripple effect seeps into our subconscious and allows for more informed choices and an appreciation of what's really important to us.

The first time I wore a scarf I had knitted out in public, it was empowering. There was no tag, and suddenly a compliment such as "I like that scarf" gave me a whole new sense of pride and accomplishment. I also didn't have to worry about anyone wearing the same thing, because even if someone else had made the same scarf from the same pattern, we would each have put our own personal stamp on it. Wearing my own creations didn't give me any sense of entitlement or superiority in the face of all the mall-bought clothes around me, but it did begin to release me from thinking that what was fashionable and best for my body shape should be dictated by trends. This led me to start making decisions on what I liked and wanted to wear versus what was available to wear. It was a giant leap into a world that further integrated craft (and craft theory) in my life. And it was welcome.

- -

Knitting for Good Actions

| Responsibility in Retail |

Think that you'd like to plan your wardrobe more ethically? Take a minute to go through the clothes in your closet that you wear most often. Where were they made? If you've never taken time to check, it can be a bit shocking to see just how many other countries are making what you're wearing. Do any of the countries surprise you?

Once you've found out where your clothes were made, have a look at the companies that made them. Try doing an Internet search on the brand of clothing and add the keywords "business practice" or "sustainability." As the public has become more aware of unethical manufacturing practices and demanded more accountability, many larger retail companies have begun explaining their business practices on their websites. If you can't find anything about a particular brand, try e-mailing the company directly about its business practices. In some cases, you may be horrified, whereas in others, you may be happy to know you're supporting a company with ethical modes of production.

| Reflecting on Handmade |

Sometimes the very process of creating something from scratch can lead to other questions. Has your knitting allowed you to consider how clothes are/should be produced? Has seeing the creation of something from start to finish allowed you to rethink any part of your life? Has it made you think about the production of household goods or makeup or processed foods? How does it feel to hold a finished handmade item in your hands?

Striped Hat for the Homeless

Designed by Linda Permann

Along with scarves, hats are another frequently requested handmade item. Linda Permann designed this striped hat as a stash-buster, so you can help the homeless and help yourself by decluttering at the same time—the pattern that follows can be made using scrap yarn you have around the house. She employed several colors, but you can play around with the width and arrangements of the stripes, incorporate novelty yarns of similar weight, or ignore the color directions altogether and knit a solid cap. It works up in just a night or two, so your commitment doesn't have to be overwhelming. Add a pom-pom or tassel for an extra heartfelt touch.

| FINISHED MEASUREMENTS |

20″ circumference (stretches to 23″)

| YARN |

Brown Sheep Company Lamb's Pride Bulky (85% wool/15% mohair; 125 yards/113 grams): a total of 1 skein made up of several colors. Use any colors you like and change the width and repetition of stripes as desired—or knit a solid hat! I used these colors, referred to in the pattern by letter: M-151 Chocolate Soufflé (A), M-02 Brown Heather (B), M-240 Prairie Goldenrod (C), M-47 Tahiti Teal (D), M-97 Rust (E), M-82 Blue Flannel (F)

| NEEDLES |

One 16″ circular (circ) needle size US 10 (6 mm)

One set double pointed needles (dpns) size US 10 (6 mm)

Change needle size if necessary to obtain correct gauge.

| NOTIONS |

Yarn needle

| GAUGE |

14 sts and 20 rows = 4″ (10 cm) in Stockinette stitch (St st)

| HAT |

With circ needle and A, CO 70 stitches. Place marker and join being careful not to twist sts.

Rnds 1–8: *K1, p1; rep from * around.

| STRIPE PATTERN |

Work in St st (k all rnds), working stripes in colors as indicated:
Rnd 9: A.
Rnds 10, 11, and 12: B
Rnd 13: C.
Rnds 14, 15, 16, and 17: D.
Rnd 18 and 19: A.
Rnds 20, 21, and 22: E.
Rnd 23: B.
Rnd 24 and 25: C.
Rnd 26: F.
Rnds 27 and 28: D.
Rnd 29: E.

| SHAPE CROWN |

Note: Switch to dpns once your hat feels tight on the circs.
With color B, work as follows:
Rnd 30: *K8, k2tog; rep from * —63 sts.
Rnd 31: *K7, k2tog; rep from * —56 sts.
Rnd 32: Knit.
Rnd 33: *K6, k2tog; rep from * —49 sts.
Rnd 34: *K5, k2tog; rep from * —42 sts.
Rnd 35: Knit.

With color A, work as follows:
Rnd 36: *K4, k2tog; rep from * —35 sts.
Rnd 37: *K3, k2tog; rep from * —28 sts.
Rnd 38: *K2, k2tog; rep from * —21 sts.
Rnd 39: *K1, k2tog; rep from * —14 sts.
Rnd 40: *K2tog around—7 sts.
Cut long tail and thread tail through needle. Draw needle through remaining stitches, pull tight. Weave in all ends.

chapter three

knitting some relief
craft as therapy

ONCE WE'VE BEEN DRAWN TO KNITTING AND COME TO APPRECIATE WHAT IT HAS GIVEN US IN A HISTORICAL AND SOCIAL CONTEXT, WE CAN BEGIN TO RELAX INTO OUR CRAFT. WE CAN SEE THE WAYS that knitting can help tame our thoughts and ease our minds. Some of the most amazing personal benefits of handcraft can't be seen or heard or touched—the therapeutic and meditative benefits. While each one of us will have different experiences in practice, the act of crafting can help us all slow down a little, think a bit more clearly, and work out some of our various emotional kinks.

Perhaps the words of the great knitter Elizabeth Zimmerman say it best in *Knitting without Tears*, "Properly practiced, knitting soothes the troubled spirit and it doesn't hurt the untroubled spirit either. When I say properly practiced, I mean executed in a relaxed manner, without anxiety, strain or tension, but with confidence, inventiveness, pleasure and ultimate pride. If you hate to knit, why, bless you, don't; follow your secret heart and take up something else. But if you start out knitting with enjoyment, you will probably continue in this pleasant path." Even though it is a humble practice, knitting can harness energy that enlivens, soothes, and heals.

A Quiet Mind: Knitting and Meditation

When I first started knitting, it felt anything but therapeutic or relaxing. My fingers fumbled clumsily trying to get two tiny sticks to do what I wanted, and for the first week or so, they never seemed to comply. For that (incredibly long) week, I wondered if I had embarked on the wrong activity as the swearwords muttered under my breath were more numerous than the rows accumulating on my needles. Much to my surprise, my hands eventually took over from my brain. Suddenly I wasn't thinking about what I was doing, my fingers seemed to be under someone else's control as they knitted and purled repeatedly with few errors. It was a moment for celebration, although I was too scared to stop in case I wouldn't know how to get started again. Things only got better after I got the fundamentals sorted out; I could never have guessed at all the benefits and surprises knitting would later bring.

Perhaps one of its most unexpected effects is its ability to help me focus my thoughts and quiet my mind as I create. Somehow my daily tensions start washing away with the rhythmic movement—hopefully this is true for you too. I find that I am able to focus on the stitch, when at most other times in my life I find myself constantly distracted. When I'm knitting, I can focus my thoughts on something refreshingly simple: wool and wood. With my hands at work, my mind and creativity are free to roam and explore.

I find this state is less about completely forgetting the world and more about letting all the annoyances and worries that rack up each day slink off and disappear as I make stitch after stitch after stitch. As the needles click, the yarn weaves through my hands, and the item I'm making grows before my eyes, there is a process of creating and releasing. Everything boils down in my busy mind to the repetition of my movements, which finally allows me to let go of whether or not I've done the laundry or washed the dishes.

Such moments of tactile respite can help set up your mind for new thoughts and plans and actions, freeing you from feeling trapped by your never-ending to-do list. By allowing a few moments for yourself and your creativity, you can give yourself a much-needed break from the chaos of daily life. This break doesn't have to be a grand act—just a simple addition to your day. For example, I often have my knitting with me around town because I find it helps bring calm to moments of angst or worry, but it wasn't always this way.

The last time I was looking for employment was in the springtime, and having no privacy in my office, I went outside for interviews. I would sit on a quiet, grassy hill nearby for a few minutes before a prospective employer was supposed to call and find myself staring at my cell phone, nervously awaiting yet another interview. On one such day, I took out my knitting after a few minutes of staring fruitlessly at the phone. I worked a few rows, paying specific attention to my breath. When the phone finally rang, I was much calmer than I had been for any of my previous interviews. By accident, I discovered that instead of waiting for worry to accumulate, I could use my knitting as a way to focus on my breath at that moment, successfully keeping my interview anxiety at bay. Since then, I have rarely been without my knitting, just in case.

Much of the meditative quality of knitting comes from its repetition. There is safety in repetition; we are likely to know the end result, so there is little anxiety in the process. According to Dr. Herbert Benson, who has spent his career researching the mind-body connection, "Benefits can come from a spectrum of repetitive, mind-clearing practices that elicit the so-called relaxation response—from swaying in prayer to saying the rosary to knitting." It was Benson who termed this the Relaxation Response, which works on the principle of getting your whole body to relax. The response itself is defined as "a physical state of deep rest that changes the physical and emotional responses to stress (e.g., decreases in heart rate, blood pressure, rate of breathing, and muscle tension)."

We can take the relaxing benefit of knitting's repetitive nature a bit further by looking at it as a meditation. When we are able to sink into the safety of our knitting and clear our minds, we can turn our focus to our breathing, deepening our experience. As Tara Jon Manning writes in her book *Mindful Knitting*, "The act of knitting is inherently built on the formation of a stitch, the creation of fabric. When we knit, we place our attention over and over again on the natural rhythm of creating fabric from yarn—insert needle, wrap yarn, pull through a new stitch, repeat. Following this simple repetitive action is the basis of contemplative practice. It continually reminds us to stay focused, to stay in the moment. When we knit with this attention, we have an almost indescribable feeling of satisfaction and contentment. This is knitting as meditation."

We can pursue this meditative aspect intentionally or set a specific time to do a knitting meditation during which we knit a simple pattern, not worrying about perfection. Sit down with your knitting and strive to knit and meditate for a certain length of time. Once that time has lapsed, cut the yarn, and rip out the work you just did. This way, the next time you want to do a knitting meditation, you can knit until the yarn runs out, marking the allotted time you wanted to meditate.

As we try to navigate our daily responsibilities, it's important that we take the time to rest and be still. Just taking a snippet of time for ourselves, when we're not running around trying to finish everything on our agendas, can actually benefit the quality of our work. In all our rushing around, we often forget that giving our minds a few minutes off can put a fresher and brighter perspective on things. The hardest part is remembering that we *deserve* a few calm moments. But where do we find them?

Even though I kept running around from one thing to the next every day, I decided to start taking my knitting with me everywhere as an experiment. On the days when I felt like I had no time to myself, the very act of getting out my knitting was a reminder of the bits and bobs of quiet I did have. Whenever I found myself waiting or traveling on the subway, I would pull out my knitting. I would sometimes work half a row, sometimes twenty, but at the end of the week, I had made progress—although admittedly more some weeks than others. And when I thought back on how hectic my week had been, I could quantify the moments I'd had to myself in the progress of my knitting. Suddenly what seemed like useless bits of free time became time spent relaxed instead of stressed. Instead of idly daydreaming or worrying about my next destination, I emptied my mind of all of it and enjoyed a few hard-earned minutes of reprieve. The added benefit of helping ease my nerves before an interview? Another wonderful surprise!

Bryant Holsenbeck

BRYANT HOLSENBECK IS AN ENVIRONMENTAL ARTIST FROM DURHAM, NORTH CAROLINA. SHE WRITES ABOUT HER LIFE, HER ARTWORK, AND EVERYTHING IN BETWEEN AT BRYANTHOLSENBECK.COM.

Since I was a child, I have been making things. The process begins when I pick up a material or an object that interests me in some way. When I was a young girl, my father was a textile engineer, and his company was developing a brand of polyester called caprolyon—the new "miracle fabric." He once brought home this stretchy, striped fabric, very much akin to modern-day fleece. I felt it and stretched it for a while, then I decided that I was going to cut some of it up and make an animal out of it. All weekend I cut and sewed, absorbed in the idea of what I was making and the form that was taking shape. In the end, I had a lumpy, elephant-looking thing and a deep sense of contentment.

In a way, when I make a book out of recycled paper and corrugated cardboard, or a crow out of scraps of fabric, old zippers, and plastic grocery bags, I am still doing what I did when I was ten years old—taking everyday materials and transforming them. In the process, I get lost in the moment and time expands. The feel of the materials I am using, the rhythm of the work (stitching, sewing, cutting, ripping, sewing, and wrapping), and a form I recognize emerging from the chaos are the gifts I get from the process of making something. This making is and has always been both a meditation and a quest. The thing that gets made—the book, the sweater, the lumpy stuffed elephant, or the crow—is the phoenix that rises from the process.

Your mind shuts off—or dials down to a more comforting rhythm. Everyone is meditating these days, which is not a bad idea at all; we need to slow ourselves down anyway we can. But I say we should also stop and sew our buttons on, make a piecrust, knit a sweater, make a book, breathe, enjoy the feel of cloth or wool in our hands and on our skin. Our hands working in the rhythm of these actions is as peaceful and as radical an act as any that I know.

Knitting through Difficult Emotions

When we consider knitting a form of meditation, we can also see it as a profound vehicle for dealing with difficult emotions. If we want to finish a craft project, we have to stick with it, whether it's going smoothly or not. If we want to work through our difficult emotions, we must stick with those also. As the American Buddhist nun Pema Chödrön suggests, sitting with our emotions—instead of trying to brush them off—can help us work them out instead of letting them accumulate. Chödrön writes in her book, *The Places That Scare You*, that by staying with our emotions, "we develop a loyalty to our experience." At times, when we feel like we can't take the chaos or hurt that surrounds us, we can sit with our knitting like we would with meditation.

By allowing our minds to work through what we're feeling while our hands follow a familiar and comforting rhythm, we allow our emotions to sink in and work their way through our bodies—from the reluctance of letting our negative feelings settle and root to acceptance of the outcome and the discovery of new paths we can take to make things better. Due to its soothing nature, knitting creates a safe space in which to sit comfortably, whether with our uncomfortable thoughts when we're feeling unsure, with our anxieties when we're nervous, or with our joy when we're happy. In turn, not only are we processing emotion, but we are producing something with our hands that documents that process. When we stick with our knitting, the outcome can be emotionally cleansing as well as visually stunning.

Sometimes I find that when I get stuck on one particular emotion and am making no headway in working through it, I'm much better off pulling out my knitting than seeking advice from friends and family (which I do mainly because I want someone to agree with me). While it may not be an instant fix, sitting and knitting with your emotions can help stagnant thoughts move on, creating more space for positive ideas.

Beyond giving us time to think and feel, knitting allows us to stay in the present. The idea of sitting and knitting with my emotions was tested for me when I was living in England. I was living on a sheep farm in the southeast, but was visiting a friend in central London when I got a phone call from my mother saying that my grandfather had passed away. I felt stranded, looking at unfamiliar faces and missing my family. I walked around the city for a while, trying to figure out how best to ride public transportation to my friend's apartment.

When I arrived there, I sat down on her couch and, without really thinking about it, pulled out my knitting. I knitted row after row after row, internalizing my grandfather's death and my sudden imminent return to America. All I could do was cry and knit and drink tea in near silence with my friend nearby, only speaking up occasionally to share a memory of my grandfather. After many, many rows, I was better able to think about the plane tickets that needed to be booked, how I was going to get back to the farm and pack, and where I was going to find something to wear to the funeral that didn't look like I had come straight off a sheep pasture in less than thirty-six hours. Even though I was still deeply saddened, by taking that time out to process what had happened, I was able to get back home quickly and without incident.

In the quiet nature of knitting, a rhythm formed as I allowed my body to soak in my sadness instead of trying to push my mind on to other things in order to ease the pain. This rhythm carried me from London to the United States, as I kept knitting and breathing and letting my emotions go where they needed to. Once I stopped trying to steer them and just let my breath and my knitting flow, my mind could finally process what was going on.

In this vein, perhaps knitting's therapeutic benefits are related to the creation of something new. Practically everything is so readily available these days that there is no need to create anything in our daily lives unless we want to. Instead of taking from the world, we are adding to it, and this positive action can help us get through difficult times. In her essay, "Our Family Heritage: A Conversation Between Two Sisters" from *Women and Craft*, Sue Pooley writes, "During [my sister's] divorce, we found that we had closed ranks with our mother in a tight support group, offering therapy in the form of an intense and prolonged period of making things for each other. During the worst three months, it seems to us now that by contriving this close triangle and sharing our handiwork, we were instinctively coming to terms with our own parts in the drama that was going on around us. Much talk, of course, went on at these times, but there seemed to be some powerful relationship between what we were doing with our hands, and the healing of our emotional wounds." Sometimes the process of knitting can be just as therapeutic as the end product (if not more so).

Felicity (Felix) Ford

FELICITY (FELIX) FORD IS AN ARTIST AND THE CREATOR OF THE MISSABILITY RADIO SHOW, WHICH REMINDS AND TEACHES LISTENERS THE DIFFERENT WAYS WE CAN THINK AND TALK ABOUT DISABILITY.

The idea is to create a collection of walking-stick cozies that challenges perceptions about disability and makes positive statements about personalization, customization and dignity.

—Publicity statement from the *Missability Radio Show*'s Knitted Walking Stick Cosy Competition

When I walked with a gray, hospital-issued walking stick, people often asked what was "wrong" with me. Equipment is an instant symbol of impairment. It can be useful for people to be able to see that you have difficulty walking, but on the other hand, sometimes that is *all* people see! When I covered my stick in green felt, people instead asked where the great stick had come from, and we talked about craft and creativity. Covering my walking stick had an empowering effect, casting me in the role of innovator, inventor, and maker.

The felted cover wore thin quickly, and I began to think about covers that could be made inexpensively and easily detached. Many people get their equipment on loan from state health services and so cannot paint the surfaces if they dislike them. Knitting has fewer disadvantages.

Knitting can be executed in the round for seamless construction. The means of making covers are also easy to share, as many people can read and adapt knitting patterns. Knitted cosies can be made inexpensively, often using as little as 25 grams (0.88 ounces) of wool. Knitted cosies don't hinder the functionality of walking aids and can be designed sensibly. Most important, knitted items can be tailor-made to suit an individual's tastes and needs.

The dignifying and affirmative potential of this last fact is enormous. Equipment is manufactured as cheaply as possible in order to save money. There is also a wish to neutralize the appearance of equipment as much as possible in a cost-cutting, one-size-fits-all approach. Increases in choice, color, and styles available would inevitably result in greater expenses for disabled people, and we cannot reasonably expect health care systems to prioritize the provision of stylish equipment over more fundamental concerns (such as reducing waiting lists for operations). The Knitted Walking Stick Cosy returns power to individuals who wish to integrate their equipment into their overall style and gives them access to colors, designs, textures, and materials that may never be commercially available.

The online knitting community is incredibly skilled, and I felt that opening up the Walking Stick Cosy contest to other makers would generate a lot more ideas and possibilities than I could come up with on my own. I also wanted to find a way of bringing together the practical considerations inherent in both equipment design and knitting. So many conversations about living with a disability or knitting a garment revolve around problem solving and ingenuity, and I wanted to bring those worlds together; to shift questions about living with a disability away from medicine and hospitals and into knitting circles everywhere.

Relief from Physical Pain

Although it may seem surprising, knitting can also help us work through physical pain. The theory of distraction is something we may have first encountered as children getting a vaccination at the doctor's office. To lessen the anxiety or perceived pain (which was often worse than the actual pain), the doctor or nurse would make a silly face or point to a cute stuffed animal. Once you were engaged with this new stimulus conveniently placed in easy view, they would swoop in with the shot, and before you realized it, it was over and you'd barely felt a thing. By allowing your mind to focus on nicer things—like fluffy stuffed animals—instead of the pain, it becomes possible to actually reduce the amount of pain you feel. Think it sounds like something only a child would fall for?

After seeing and hearing about how stitching can be beneficial to people who are ill, Betsan Corkhill started StitchLinks.com in 2003. This online forum provides a safe place for people who stitch and have chronic pain or illness to write and dialogue about the relationship between craft and pain relief.

Betsan says, "StitchLinks was born because I believed there was/is a large gap in health care that should be filled. It appears from anecdotal evidence collected from knitters worldwide that knitting can fill this gap to provide an effective tool to complement medical treatments and as a tool for preventive care. I believe this even more strongly now." According to the website, knitting and stitching help distract individuals from their pain or condition by creating a needed distraction. Research has proven that "distraction is one of the most powerful analgesics we know of and that brain centers responsible for releasing the body's natural opioids are stimulated during distraction." Knitting and stitching allow for gentle concentration and diversion, giving "a person control over their condition, which can significantly change their outlook on life. They keep the hands and mind occupied." One of the important facets of StitchLinks is that not only does it provide a link to information on the therapeutic nature of stitching, but it also provides emotional support. Notes Betsan, "The psychological support they receive from other members is vitally important both for improving their knitting skills and also in managing their medical conditions. Many who suffer from long-term medical conditions have low self-esteem and low social confidence. Being able to talk to people who have had similar experiences makes a huge difference." By providing this unique forum, StitchLinks aids many makers in learning how to get more out of their needlework.

Whether or not such a website is for you, getting absorbed in an activity—be it knitting or embroidery or woodworking—just might be beneficial to your health. Definitely something worth remembering the next time someone chastises you for being distracted by your handwork!

While research is ongoing to prove scientifically that there is a connection between pain relief and stitching, work done by Hunter Hoffman using virtual reality environments with burn patients presents more information about why distraction can help us work through pain or anxiety. Reporting on Hoffman's findings, an article in the *American Pain Society Bulletin* states that playing a virtual reality game can make "less attention available to process incoming pain signals. Conscious attention is required for the experience of pain." While knitting is far from a virtual reality game, it can absorb your attention in much the same way, especially when you're reading a difficult pattern or learning a new technique. As your concentration is diverted away from how your body is feeling and toward your project, you have fewer thoughts about any pain or discomfort you are experiencing.

The personal effects of knitting may not be what brought you to the craft in the first place, but it is definitely an added benefit. When you are aware and open, knitting can give you time to be meditative and still, to process emotion, and to take a respite from any physical pain—while you're also producing a tangible outcome. Sometimes the pace of life can be so frantic it seems like there's never an appropriate time to just be. There are moments to rush and hurry, and moments to sit and absorb everything. It's in these moments of stillness, when you're quietly working your craft, when you can be in the moment with clarity and insight.

Knitting for Good Actions

| Breathing with the Stitch |

If you find knitting relaxing, try consciously meditating while you're doing it, aligning your breath with the stitches. The pace of your knitting and breathing is up to you. What's important here is establishing a rhythm that allows you to slow down your breath and focus more on the actions of your hands.

| Staying with Emotion |

If you haven't yet used your knitting as a way to work through emotional and physical pain, try turning to it the next time you have a strong emotional response to a situation and need/have time to work through how to best handle it. I bet you'll be surprised at what solutions you come up with after just a few rows.

Basket-weave Baby Blanket

Designed by Kelly Wooten

One of the best ways to work through emotional upheaval is to tackle a project that has enough repetition to help you collect your thoughts, but not so much that you get bored. Baby blankets are another item frequently needed at various charities and can be a great comfort to little ones.

| FINISHED MEASUREMENTS |

48" x 48"

Note: To make a different size blanket, add or subtract a multiple of 14 sts to the number of CO sts. Every 14 sts will change the blanket size by 3".

| YARN |

Brown Sheep Company Serendipity Tweed (60% cotton/40% wool; 210 yards/100 grams): 5 skeins #ST12 Water Lily Leaves

| NEEDLES |

One 36" circular needle size US 8 (5 mm)

Change needle size if necessary to obtain correct gauge.

| NOTIONS |

2 stitch markers

| GAUGE |

18 sts and 24 rows = 4" (10 cm) in Stockinette stitch (St st)

| BOTTOM BORDER |

CO 239 sts.

Rows 1–6: Knit.

Row 7: K7, place marker (M), p to last 7 sts, place M, p3, k4.

Row 8: K7, sl M, k to next M, sl M, p3, k4.

Row 9: K7, sl M, p to next M, sl M, p3, k4.

Row 10: K4, p3, sl M, p to next M, sl M, p3, k4

| Body of Blanket |

Rows 1 and 3: K7, sl M, *p12, k2; rep from * to last st before M, p1, sl M, k7.

Row 2: K4, p3, sl M, k1, *p2, k12; rep from * to M, sl M, p3, k4.

Row 4: K4, p3, sl M, p to M, sl M, p3, k4.

Rows 5, 7, 9, 11, and 13: K7, sl M, p1, *k2, p1, [k1, p1] 4 times, k2, p1; rep from * to M, sl M, k7.

Row 6, 8, 10, 12, and 14: K4, p3, sl M, k1 *p3, k1, [p1, k1] 3 times, p3, k1; rep from * to M, sl M, p3, k4.

Rows 15 and 17: K7, sl M, p1, *k2, p12; rep from * to M, sl M, k7.

Row 16: K4, p3, sl M, *k12, p2; rep from * to last st before M, k1, sl M, p3, k4.

Row 18: K4, p3, sl M, p to M, sl M, p3, k4.

Rep rows 1–18 a total of 19 times or to desired length.

| Top Border |

Rows 1 and 3: K4, p3, sl M, p to M, sl M, k7.

Row 2: K4, p3, sl M, k to M, sl M, k7.

Row 4: K4, p3, sl M, p to M, sl M, p3, k4.

Row 5–10: Knit.

Bind off knitwise.

part two knitting *for* your community

chapter four

----

using craft to connect
building communities through common bonds

WHEN I WAS A CHILD, I USED TO DREAM ABOUT THE HOUSE I'D LIVE IN, WHOM I'D LIVE NEAR, AND THE COMMUNITY WHERE I'D CHOOSE TO LIVE MY LIFE WHEN I GREW UP. AT THE TIME, ADULTHOOD FELT LIKE IT WOULD never come and all of those choices were so far away. But adulthood did come. And even as an adult, the dreamworld of television had me seriously thinking that when you moved somewhere new, your neighbors would always welcome you with open arms (and if you're really lucky, with pie). Unfortunately, despite moving more than thirty times, I have never once been met with baked goods.

For many of us, this sense of community—where the neighbors know each other and welcome wagons are the norm—exists only on television. As the majority of us live our lives in neighborhoods where we don't know our neighbors, more often than not, we don't want to bother anyone during the few spare minutes they have at home or have anyone bother us. To make up for the lack of a geographic community, we find ourselves creating a community of friends and acquaintances apart from our neighborhoods—people from work or places we volunteer—hoping that it will make up for the fact that we don't know the name of the guy next door whose stereo is up too loud late at night. But that's not how it needs to be, because we *live our lives* in our neighborhoods. Connection to the community is the first step in having a positive effect on those around us. Being able to greet our neighbors by name enables us to better understand the true meaning of "home."

I don't believe it's a matter of us not wanting to engage in our communities; it's a matter of not really knowing how to do it. But chances are you can turn one of your current interests into a vehicle that facilitates a community connection—your community just might need you as much as you need it. In this chapter, we start small by connecting with family and friends, then push our focus outward to meet new people.

Starting a Conversation: Knitting as a Common Language

Although I knew that I had gained a lot personally from knitting, I had no idea that it could be beneficial to my relationships with others. I've taught crafts in the various communities I've lived in and have seen how knitting can help students relate to people they don't know. But the real extended value of connecting to strangers didn't hit home in earnest until I saw how it allowed a closeness to develop in my long-term relationship with a relative, even though we had previously had little in common.

My Great-aunt Gene is always at our annual family beach week and the occasional relative-related weddings and funerals. Even though I like to think that I can talk to anyone, for the first thirty years of my life, I was never really sure what to talk about with Aunt Gene. We would chat about the weather, food, how kids in the family had grown, but we never quite found a way to have a conversation of any real substance or depth. It wasn't until I happened to take out my knitting in front of her one day that we began to communicate seriously. Although I had met people and had hundreds of discussions about knitting with strangers in both the United States and the United Kingdom, my first real conversation with Aunt Gene was no doubt the most rewarding. Her face became animated, and her eyes sparkled as she started talking about all the sweaters she knits for her twenty-odd grandchildren and great-grandchildren each Christmas and how she also taught the nuns in her local parish to knit.

Having my knitting out in the open helped us find some common ground. Our conversation had a firm starting point—what I was making—and then slowly moved on to other topics. Now Aunt Gene and I talk about things besides knitting; it just took a scarf still on the needles to start things off.

Thanks to the positive changes in my relationship with my aunt, I have come to refer to the "Aunt Gene theory" whenever I make connections with people in my community via my creativity. Through teaching, I was given the opportunity to see a transformation occur for the duration of each lesson. Having seen the dynamics of a familial relationship change over time, I began to understand that there are benefits to knitting with others beyond just teaching them something new and then setting them free. We can have conversations that unfold just like the knitting itself. Instead of only speaking for a minute in passing, when you are knitting with someone else, you have a chance to see where a conversation takes you without having to rush. Just as your knitting has a rhythm, so do the conversations you engage in while you work. The ease of conversation prompted by craft helps us connect with others beyond our own racial, economic, or social backgrounds, allowing everyone involved to learn about someone new and foster a sense of belonging.

Whenever I start thinking that I'm not making any difference, I remember my very unscientific theory and press on, knowing my community is to be lived in—not ignored until it blends into the background.

One of the benefits of handmade is that by doing something like knitting or wearing a handmade item in public, we provide a topic for conversation with people who have similar interests. I've been stopped on the subway by a person who liked my hat and have struck up a conversation with someone when I noticed that the sweater she was wearing comprised the exact same stitch pattern as a sock I had recently finished.

Crafts like knitting, which are considered "different" yet culturally familiar activities, help us facilitate conversations. Try knitting in public or letting your knitting needles stick out of the top of your bag as you travel about town. I can almost guarantee that some sort of conversation will present itself. See how it feels, and then see where it goes.

There are other things you can carry with you that can also act as conversation starters (a baby and a puppy come instantly to mind), but few portable activities embody a skill that has been carried down through generations all over the world like knitting does. It may seem a little silly, but in its own gentle way, this seemingly simple craft can help you connect to your neighbors. It may even show you a whole new part of your community that you didn't know existed.

Diane Gilleland

DIANE GILLELAND PRODUCES CRAFTYPOD.COM, A BLOG AND PODCAST ABOUT MAKING STUFF. SHE ALSO RUNS DIYALERT.COM, A WEBSITE ABOUT THE CRAFTY CULTURE IN HER HOMETOWN OF PORTLAND, OREGON.

One of the most powerful things about the act of making (in my opinion, anyway) is the way it connects us to each other. Take two strangers, put something crafty in their hands, and before long, they'll be chatting away like old friends. There's something about the relaxed and joyful mental state we fall into when we make things—it vaults us right over our social inhibitions and into real communication.

This was what I had in mind when I started a chapter of the Church of Craft in my hometown of Portland, Oregon. I wanted our meetings to create a safe place where anyone could come, sit down at a table with strangers, and make friends through a few hours of crafting.

Why is that important? Because our culture tends to foster isolation. We communicate with each other via keyboards rather than face-to-face. Many cities offer precious few venues where like-minded people can meet, outside of the workplace and bars. And while we may want to meet more people, let's face it, most of us harbor a little social anxiety. It's always easier to stay home with our knitting and the TV.

And yet, there's nothing like real human connection to bring us out of ourselves and our problems, and to create fresh perspective and inspiration. Truly, we need to meet each other, if only to remind ourselves that we're not alone in the world.

On a more practical scale, there's the whole idea of "social capital," which points out that the more people you know, the more resources you have for exchanging skills, tools, and knowledge. In times of economic or social hardship, our connections to each other have very concrete value.

At our Church of Craft meetings, all this begins with a little messing about with glue and buttons (or yarn and needles, or paper and scissors). I've watched this progression time and again: People arrive at a meeting, sit down at the table, and spend the first half-hour or so ignoring each other. Then the crafting seems to relax everyone, and pretty soon, someone will offer a "Wow! I love that yarn you're using," or a "How do you get your paper to fold like that?" By the end of the meeting, the whole table is talking about everything under the sun and exchanging e-mail addresses. It's magical.

Is it world-changing? Well, I like to think of it as a kind of viral experience. If someone makes good connections at a Church of Craft meeting, then perhaps he or she will be more open to chatting with that person at the bus stop. Or getting involved in a local food drive. Or offering to carry groceries for an elderly neighbor. Real community is built on small acts like these.

Building a Craft Community

Just as family relations can be strengthened by knitting, friendships can deepen as well. By building a community of friends—those people who understand us for who we really are—we can create an environment that gives us the social safety net to try new ideas. At the best of times, this community is a group of your closest friends; at worst, it's a motley crew of individuals who make you feel a little less alone in a specific geographic area. In either case, bonds are easily formed and tightened through the knowledge of skill or interest in a hobby.

But what if you are new to the area or none of your friends share your interest? By no means are you destined to be all alone because you don't know anybody; you just have to step a little farther out into your community to get things happening. One way of doing so is to start your own knitting or craft circle.

Historically, the notion of a craft circle was quite common. It was only natural that groups of people (usually women) came together to meet for quilting bees or sewing circles or knitting groups. Of early craft groups, theorist and scholar Julia Kehew notes, "In the colonial period, spinning, weaving, knitting, and sewing were really ubiquitous parts of women's daily lives.

When they went to visit neighbors, they took their knitting or sewing. When they sat down in the evenings, they took up their knitting or sewing, or went to their wheels or looms. So in the earliest periods of American history, the social aspect of getting together with other people was really the most important thing, and the handwork that got done at the same time was incidental." Such gatherings reinforced the idea of community and allowed for the sharing of techniques and discussions about personal lives that drifted in during quiet moments. Not only time for sharing and gossiping, these social occasions were also times for showing off. Words of encouragement and approval were passed along by those who were worthy judges of skill. While the community members came together for support, they were also creating a kind of not-competitive arena, not necessarily because they were trying to show one another up, but because they wanted to test out new ideas and combinations, see how they matched up to others, and learn how new techniques could fit into their own craft repertoires.

As these groups were noncompetitive, tricks that were admired were often shared, thus allowing the skill circle to grow as those tips were passed along to still others outside of or new to the group. In times when women tended not to work outside the home (such as the early half of the twentieth century), their needlework gave them a sense of pride and accomplishment. Unlike traditional workplaces where it was always better to be one step ahead of the competition, women's skill sets improved through sharing and not being limited by their skill level or breadth of knowledge. When there were few opportunities for women to show off their skills, having a place where their needlework was praised, as well as having the chance to share their knowledge, gave them satisfaction and helped them develop self-worth. Craft circles were also especially helpful in times when women were still responsible for keeping their loved ones warm.

Today, after years of fighting for gender independence and trying to escape from the kitchen, the knitting group is making a valiant return. Some groups meet publicly, some privately, some a bit of both. But the most important thing about the knitting circle is that women (along with some needle-savvy men) are meeting. Debbie Stoller's 2003 book, *Stitch 'n Bitch*, notes that "the percentage of women under forty-five who knit or crochet has doubled since 1996." Stoller's book brought more public attention to both knitting and knitting circles, and after its publication, meetings were held with even more frequency in knitters' homes, at universities, in cafés, in bookstores, and in bars in countless towns and cities across the country.

In her research on gender and feminism, sociologist Alison Better writes, "Perhaps this is our generation's answer to the consciousness raising groups of 1970s feminism. Knitting groups, like other groups of like-minded women assembled in shared joys or struggles, provide members with social opportunities, as well as opportunities to relax, network, and share knowledge."

After high school or college, the opportunity to socialize with a group of women without the presence of a menu or a significant (nonknitting) other occurs less and less frequently as the workday lengthens. I started my knitting group by sending out an e-mail to anyone I knew who might want to participate and then held a cookout at my house to gauge people's interest over veggie burgers. It went over so well that when I suggested we meet every two weeks, the group quickly decided that meeting every week would be better! It was amazing to discover how much we all craved such gatherings—and had for years—but thought we were alone in those cravings. Better also notes, "I think today, for women who have come of age with feminism, that the domestic is being reclaimed in subversive ways. Women (and others) today are not engaging with crafts out of necessity (few are knitting to keep their families warm), they are finding joy and relaxation in shared time with friends." Thankfully craft has provided us with an excuse to spend some quality time with our friends where we can be open, honest, and relaxed and simultaneously learning new things.

When the days get hectic, there is comfort in knowing that once a week or month, there is a specific time cut out solely for making something with your hands. Not time for mending or darning or fixing life's rips and tears, but time just for creating something new with other people. Though the cultural climate has changed a lot over the decades, the companionship, skill sharing, and community gained from crafting with like-minded people is still important.

Susan Beal

SUSAN BEAL IS A WRITER AND CRAFTER IN PORTLAND, OREGON, AND THE AUTHOR OF *BEAD SIMPLE*. SHE ALSO COWROTE *SUPER CRAFTY*, AND KEEPS A DAILY CRAFT BLOG AT WESTCOASTCRAFTY.COM.

A few years ago, I started volunteering to teach art at a Portland alternative school after the school system cut all art and music classes out of the budget for grades K through 8. Figuring out how best to stretch my $30 budget (and the unpredictable and random assortment of donated art supplies that was up for grabs) over an entire semester was quite a challenge, but teaching my fifth graders each week was so rewarding. I loved my own childhood art classes so much that volunteering felt like the most natural way to give back some of my creative energy.

Now, with work and family commitments keeping me busier and busier, I'm sad to say that I don't have as much time to dedicate to craftivism that takes me out of my studio. So I've started organizing small fund-raisers for causes I believe in—lately, selling my handmade jewelry in limited editions online, and dedicating the money to organizations like Planned Parenthood or United for Peace and Justice. I also love to donate my work to online or local benefits that other people organize, and I post about any and all creative fund-raisers I want to support on my craft blog, West Coast Crafty, to help spread the word.

I'm constantly inspired by my friends, like Faythe Levine, who raises money for her *Handmade Nation* documentary through an Etsy shop; Jennifer McMullen, who donates a percentage of her sales in her Dishy Duds shop to relief efforts in Darfur; and Cathy Pitters of Bossa Nova Baby, who tirelessly volunteers to help with art events and classes at her son's elementary school. So many

Gathering Others in Your Community

All this talk of gathering friends is great, but if none of your friends are interested, it's worth trying to find a group of other knitters. If you live somewhere rural that doesn't really have a central locus, try putting flyers up at work, your church, or your community center saying that you would like to start a knitting group. If you are likely to get responses from people you don't know personally, you can always plan to meet up in a coffee shop or bookstore.

If you live in an active town or city (large or small, it doesn't matter), I suggest getting more personal. Tell everyone you know that you're looking for people to knit with. Send an e-mail to your local friends, and pass the word to coworkers and neighbors and anyone else you know. Ask them to pass it on to people they think might be interested. Chances are high that you will discover some people already in your life who knit in secret, as well as some you don't know and never would have pegged as knitters. In other words, stop telling yourself that no one will be interested in setting up some sort of craft group. Asking around and seeing who responds is part of the magic—discovering people with similar tastes outside of your usual social circle. In expanding beyond the "usual suspects," you might be pleasantly surprised at just who you meet.

Another method of starting up a group is through direct action—taking a portable knitting project with you as you go throughout your day. Not only will moments crop up where you're unexpectedly bored and waiting (so pulling out your knitting can help you center instead of becoming impatient), but people will crop up too. Often, the people who comment on your knitting are knitters themselves, or they know a knitter and have tips about local knitting resources and knitting groups. You may also get a story or two about people's memories of knitting. Over the years, I've listened to countless stories of someone learning to knit as a child or watching a relative knit items for wear. I never get tired of hearing them. At first it may seem bizarre, but in reality it's doing what people have done for centuries, allowing you to get to know individuals in your community instead of walling yourself off.

If these options seem daunting, there is always the Internet. Try doing a search for "knitting" or "knitting group" and the name of your town or community.

Taking Your Knitting to the Streets

Just as many of us feel disconnected from the people in our community, we can also feel disconnected from our physical surroundings. Get acquainted with your environment by practicing random acts of crafting. Personalize your neighborhood, and in turn, find a way to better engage with your neighbors. While the streets of your town might look a little boring, groups like Knitta—which started in Houston, Texas—show that there are (legal!) ways of making things a little more beautiful.

Started by two women with small children who never had time to knit anything big, Knitta gussied up its town by knitting cozies for light posts, street signs, and car antennae. By bringing craft to the streets we see every day, we can remind ourselves that our communities are our own, and they don't have to be one long stretch of metal, concrete, and wood. We can individualize and soften the streets we traverse and expand the notion of "home." We should be comfortable and cozy in our own communities, because after all, they exist because of our very presence within them. And if there's one thing almost all cities can use, it's a little bit of tender loving care.

While I have never knitted a cozy for a streetlight, I have participated in various acts of public knitting. My first experience was with the Cast Off Knitting Club in the fall of 2003. I had just moved to London, and by sheer luck, the craft resurgence was just beginning to blow up in Britain. This group, started by Rachael Matthews and Amy Plant, organized meetings and lessons in the unlikeliest of places, causing people to rethink the limits of craft by making them think about craft in the first place. While they had started the club several years previously to promote the joys and pleasures of knitting, the enormous public response allowed them to take knitting to places and people they hadn't imagined. They knitted in clubs, bars, subways, festivals, and parks. In the spring of 2004, Cast Off organized Craft Rocks! at the Victoria & Albert Museum in London, successfully managing to drag out several thousand people to try a bit of knitting in public.

One of the benefits of social engagement is that you knock people out of their routine and make them notice things they would normally overlook. You get them to stop and say, "I've never seen that before," instead of looking down at their feet as they normally do. When you see a light pole with a knitted band of bright colors around it, you notice the pole itself instead of letting it blend into the background. Our daily activities can become so banal that we go on autopilot, but public acts of crafting can add a little prettiness to our surroundings and spotlight things we usually miss.

By making our surroundings a little more beautiful, we claim responsibility for our environment. Katie Aaberg offers a perfect example of individualizing public spaces. To make her community in Oregon more personable and inviting, Aaberg started creating tiny paintings on cardboard and taping them to street signs in her neighborhood. She believes that "it is up to people, especially in an urban environment, to take steps to beautify their surroundings. I love taking walks and seeing people's interesting front yards or how they've decorated their houses. But other areas need beautification as well." Different cities have different personalities and ticks. "Coming from an extremely urban environment (Oakland, California) that was visually cluttered by advertising everywhere I looked, I was always grateful when some artist had taken the time/money/energy to make something interesting to look at and just left it there for others to enjoy. There's also a great power in anonymous art drops: they could be done by anyone, and you don't know who did it. You're left to wonder, who did this?"

The most important thing is to do no harm while engaging in your community. Enjoy it. Make it yours. Make it a prettier place to work and play and love. Cities and towns and villages are organisms in themselves—they have a pulse, and like us, sometimes they just need a little extra attention.

Defining Your Community When You're Always on the Move

Some of us, due to circumstance or choice, are always on the move. We go from place to place to place, and we are experts at packing quickly and fitting everything in the car. But what does that mean to our sense of community? Where is it? If you are someone who moves a lot, now is the time to sit down and consider how the concept of community applies to your situation.

Think of your community on a larger scale. Find something that energizes you that you can share. Work toward using that gift for the greater good, whether your community is your block or the whole planet. I move so often that sometimes there are long stretches where my geographic community is little more than a place where I rest my head for a few months. Those are the times when I make items for a cause I believe in and center myself in the global community. They are also the times when I remind myself that even though I may think I am without community, I never am. You might find yourself moving, but that doesn't mean you need to lose touch with the people and world around you.

If you're transient, do what you can while you're in one place, even though you may not be able to commit to weekly shifts somewhere or schedule anything too far in the future. It was in my transient years that I learned how the fluidity of community has been redefined by the Internet. With the ease of online communication allowing me to keep up with friends and causes, I realized that even though I had resisted it, I had been collecting a new sort of community even as I moved. I had amassed friends who were volunteering and doing good for others both locally and globally, all of which served to enhance my commitment to work toward a more positive planet. I finally realized that all my traveling and learning had taught me that city walls are as fluid as we choose to make them. We can work to make things better in our own backyard or in another country.

Do I think that getting involved in your local community is important and vital? Yes and yes. There is nothing like showing up to volunteer at an animal adoption center and meeting people who share your interests. It's like rediscovering where you live each time, without having to move; it's recreating that wish and craving I had for new experiences when I kept moving. But I also think there are alternative ways to view your community. You can help people who aren't highly visible. You can help those who have endured the same unfortunate life events you have. You can help just because.

Whether it's your block, your town, or another continent, your community is where you find communion and where you feel at home. It just may take you some time to figure out what its boundaries are. As my community boundaries extend across international borders, I am more convinced than ever that engaging with community (especially in a creative capacity) benefits us all and is activism in its purest form.

No matter how we go about it—whether we choose to meet with family and friends or to put out a call to see who's interested—public crafting lets us connect to our community and, most important, lets us grow. And no matter how we define our community, we can better connect with it by further exploring our creativity. This connection can be grounding.

Knitting for Good Actions

| Take That Knitting Public |

Knit somewhere in public. It's nowhere near as daunting as eating at a table for one, so you're bound to conquer this! Knit in nearby parks or cafés or on public transportation. Take your knitting with you to lectures or if you're going to be waiting in line at the post office. The idea here is to just get out and about in your own community.

| Cozy Up Your Community |

Want to gussy something up, but don't know how? Try following Knitta's example and go after places in your city. Find tree branches you can tag or signposts that need some cheering up. Is there an abandoned car on your street that's an eyesore? It might just need a little creative attention. The best way to get ideas is by driving around and noticing the lack of color in one area or another. Remember, our cities are our own.

Little 'n' Large Cushion Cover

Designed by Aneeta Patel

Know anyone who is bedridden or housebound and might need some cheering up? Sometimes people in hospitals or retirement homes need a little comfort in those dreary beds. What better way to liven up a room than a bright, soft pillow?

This versatile pattern from Aneeta Patel is knitted with a basket-weave stitch pattern and can be used to make a chunky cushion or a scented knit pillow for your linen closet. You use the same pattern, just different yarn, needles, and filling, depending on whether you're making the large or small version.

| FINISHED MEASUREMENTS |

Large Cushion: 12" x 12"
Small Pillow: 4" x 4"

| YARN |

Large Cushion: Rowan Big Wool (100% merino wool; 87 yards/100 grams): 2 skeins
Small Pillow: Any DK-weight yarn (50 grams)

| NEEDLES |

Large Cushion: One pair straight needles size US 17 (12 mm)

Small Pillow: One pair straight needles size US 6 (4 mm)
Change needle size if necessary to obtain correct gauge.

| NOTIONS |

Large Cushion: Three large buttons 1 1/2" in diameter, yarn needle, cushion pad 2–4" larger than the finished cushion cover so that the knitting stretches tightly over the pad. (This will show off the basket-weave to its best advantage.)
Small Scented Pillow: Three small

buttons 1 1/2″ in diameter, dried lavender or potpourri, an old pair of tights or socks, yarn needle

| GAUGE |

Large Cushion: 8 sts and 12 rows = 4″ (10 cm) in pattern stitch
Small Pillow: 22 sts and 30 rows = 4″ (10 cm) in pattern stitch

| LARGE CUSHION AND SMALL PILLOW |

CO 24 sts.
Rows 1–5: *K4, p4; rep from *.

Key to diagram:
.... Fold lines
● ● ● Button holes

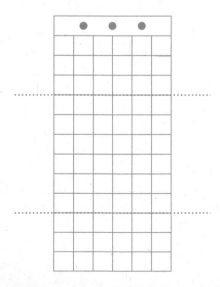

Rows 6–10: *P4, k4; rep from *.
Rep rows 1–10 a total of 6 times or to desired length.

Next row, buttonhole row: K4, [yo, k2tog, k5] twice, yo, k2tog, k4.
K 1 row. Bind off knitwise.
Weave in ends.

| FINISHING |

With wrong side facing up, fold piece at fold lines (see chart) with the short ends in the middle. Sew side seams with back stitch. Turn piece right side out. Sew on 3 buttons opposite buttonholes.

Large Cushion: Insert cushion pad into cover, pulling tight on the buttons to close.
Small Pillow: Cut the foot off an old pair of tights and fill it with potpourri or dried lavender and sew closed. Use this to stuff pillow.

Reprinted from: *Knitty Gritty: For the Absolute Beginner,* ©Aneeta Patel. Published by A&C Black in 2008. Reprinted by permission.

chapter five

reaching out to organizations

SO NOW YOU KNOW *WHY* YOU SHOULD CONNECT WITH YOUR COMMUNITY, BUT DO YOU KNOW *HOW?* TRYING TO BALANCE HOME, WORK, FAMILY, AND FRIENDS CAN MAKE THINGS DIFFICULT TO SAY THE least. But it's in moments of teaching and learning that we grow and learn and pass on our own energy. This positive symbiotic relationship also helps to strengthen our societal and familial ties. As we discussed in the last chapter, looking at creativity as a way to connect with people can allow us to shed light on parts of our environment that we may never have seen before or have overlooked.

Knowing a skill, such as knitting, provides us with a wonderful tool to help the people we don't know in our communities. By volunteering our time, knowledge, and attention to those who need it, we're doing a service to our neighborhood and ourselves. Although the following examples are just the tip of the iceberg, you can use them as a starting point for deciding where you'd like to help.

Knittin' with the Kids

For years after I graduated from college, I labored under the mistaken belief that, in modern parlance, I was "down with the kids." As I get older, I realize that with each year I age, the further I get from being able to relate to them on a cultural level. I'm convinced that everyone must go through that rite of passage when they find themselves singing loudly and off-key to an anthem from their youth only to turn around and have someone much younger ask, "*What* is that?"

After several misguided attempts at trying to connect with younger people, I tried what I had tried many times before, I pulled out my knitting. It turns out that the opportunity to create something with really long string and pointy things is much more enticing to children than impromptu lessons on seemingly arcane music. I discovered that if you have the opportunity to teach a child to knit, you have unearthed a serious creative gold mine. When children start working those needles, there's no telling what will come out of it.

Lest you think giving young children semipointy needles and a skein of yarn is an accident waiting to happen, students who go to Waldorf schools learn how to knit as part of their first-grade curriculum. Knitting is believed to aid hand-eye coordination and keeping track of stitch patterns makes counting an action, so these little ones are encouraged to follow their creativity from a very young age.

I have learned through trial and error, so when I teach knitting, I now know to start out by likening the knitting needles to chopsticks, leading the children toward the notion that these tiny sticks will be put to use for a specific task. After the general hand positions have been reviewed and the knit stitch has been taught, I leave the little knitters-in-training on their own for a while; they always pick up the craft at an astronomically faster rate than adults. The moment when they realize they're making something real and tangible, as well as that they can make whatever they want, is an epiphany. Their creative force is unleashed, and without fear of judgment or failure, they create just to *create*. There is no "right way" that something should look once children have a vision in their heads of what they're creating, it's just wrapping and looping and watching their creations grow. Whereas adults tend to think ahead of themselves, children think about what they can make at that very moment and how they can manipulate the yarn differently to create new stitches from the one they've just learned. In other words, they feel free to go completely off the map.

Through the years I've taught numerous children to knit, even in the most unusual of places. All the scenarios tend to be similar to the day I taught a chili champion's daughter to knit in the North Carolina heat. My friend Barbara, who is always crafty in the cleverest of ways, had asked me to accompany her (and her pineapple chicken chili) to a local chili cook-off. I was entirely too curious to say no. After a while, I pulled out my knitting and soon noticed a girl of around nine or ten inching away from her dad, the chili champion, and closer my way to see what I was doing. I asked, "Do you know how to knit?" to which she answered, "No." When I asked whether she would like to learn, she responded adamantly, "I can't do that. It looks too hard." When I pulled out an extra skein and needles from my bag, she couldn't resist. Within no time, we were off; she picked up the knit stitch in less than five minutes. When it was time for the chili cook-off results, she stopped knitting, I cast off her work, and she ran over to her dad's tent. Beaming, she said, "Look what I made!" The brilliance of her smile made the chili seem bland in comparison.

Teaching a child to knit is just a small way to pass along the tradition of knitting and to share that creative spark we all cherish. Sometimes it just takes a little energy and passion to light some fires. I'm always excited when I get the chance to work with kids because I know I can dance and sing and play and create. I also know that I'm making a positive difference when I see the smiles on their faces as we knit and learn together.

By existing in the moment, sitting down with yarn and needles in hand, unconcerned about what's for supper or if the electricity bill has been paid, these children become petite reminders of how finding the "now" can help us to create without a pattern, to plunge in with just with our knowledge and imagination as resources. We can use this same energy when we work with others in our community besides kids, taking note of our experiences with younger pupils and applying that knowledge accordingly. The important part of investing some of your creative skills in your community is that not only will others get the chance to learn something new, but you will learn and grow as well.

Kari Falk

THINK KIDS DON'T BELIEVE KNITTING IS COOL? KARI FALK TEACHES A FI-
BERS CLASS FOR MIDDLE SCHOOL STUDENTS.

I teach a fibers/weaving class for eighth graders, and there have been as many boys as girls (or perhaps more) taking the class. I have even been told that one of these boys has taken to knitting while his science teacher talks to the class. He still is an A student, so she doesn't seem to mind. I also have had students get their family members involved in knitting.

I know that a number of my students in the past have found that art is an acceptable way to express themselves to others without fear of rejection. Teaching seventh and eighth graders can be hard, and it is usually difficult for them to see what is really good for them. At least when it comes from what I am teaching them, many kids tell me that they didn't realize how much they learned until they have moved to the next level! I usually teach the students the basics of knitting and encourage them to go further.

Knitting with the Elderly

Since many women now in their seventies and beyond learned to knit at a young age, they can be unique knitting companions within your community. Volunteering to knit with someone in a retirement home who doesn't have many visitors may give you a chance to see what knitting is like with a person outside of your usual circle while simultaneously making that person's day. By combining companionship and skill sharing in one activity, there is a mutual benefit to knitting while you volunteer, resulting in a simultaneous zap to the creativity of everyone involved.

Much of my current work owes a great debt to the women of previous generations. Learning crafts has taught me more about how women clothed and warmed their families for hundreds of years, has allowed me to get closer to my older female relatives, and has increased my respect and appreciation for those who came before me. Many of them have so much to teach us, but we take and don't think of giving back. Sometimes just spending your time listening to people talk can do untold wonders, especially when they may not have had anyone to talk to for quite a while.

If you can't engage with any elderly relatives or neighbors, see if there are any senior centers, retirement homes, or hospitals in your area that would like volunteers to spend time with the elderly in their facilities. Realizing how little effort it can take to make people light up is as heartbreaking as it is inspiring, but that only means that what you're doing is very great indeed.

Making the Invisible Visible

On the fringes of our communities are those people we don't see by design: the incarcerated, the homeless, the hungry, the mentally ill, even homeless animals. While these groups are perhaps furthest from our consciousness, as well as our everyday dealings, they are the ones who can perhaps use our help the most.

Helping the invisible members of our society engage in craft brings them to our attention. Instead of being tucked away, their crafted items say that creativity isn't limited and that people who are homeless, forgotten, or in prison have ideas and concerns just like the rest of us. They cannot only learn new things, but they can make pretty things to boot.

Prisoners

One thing that people in prison have is loads of time, and as anyone who has ever knitted anything larger than a hat can tell you, knitting takes time. Prisoners may seem like an odd third choice after children and the elderly. However, there are many examples of the good prisoners are doing with craft as they pay their respective debts to society.

One program that believes prisoners can benefit from learning a new skill is England's Fine Cell Work, an organization that teaches needlework to inmates. The participants in this program benefit in numerous ways: they learn something new, which brings a sense of pride; their pieces are sold, which brings them a source of income; and in perfecting their needlework and embroidery, they acquire a skill they can use once they return to the outside world.

The juxtaposition of gritty prison life with pretty embroidered pillows seems a bit unlikely at first, but in a world where every day can seem the same, the ability to watch a piece of needlework grow can be a welcome accomplishment. And being able to use their energy in a positive and creative direction can help prisoners gain a sense of pride in what they're learning and making.

Hardened inmates don't seem like individuals who would dare find themselves sitting down to needlepoint a pillow or knit a hat for an infant. But I believe this view comes more from our own stereotypes than anything else. We perceive inmates as people who would be unable to sit down and create something worthy of being called beautiful. But just as not everyone who knits is humble and sweet, not everyone in the prison system is hard and gruff. These are both constructs that we've created to make the order of life easier to understand. Inmates, as much as anyone else, can benefit from craft.

Heather Cameron

HEATHER CAMERON IS AN ART THERAPIST AND ARTIST LIVING IN VANCOUVER, CANADA. ON HER WEBSITE, TRUESTITCHES.COM, SHE WRITES ABOUT CRAFT AND COMMUNITY.

I have always made things. Up until fairly recently, however, I had only knitted, embroidered, or spun yarn on my own. I knew the pleasure and satisfaction that came from creating something with my own hands, had experienced the deep, peaceful calm of gentle, repetitive movements.

In 2002, I began training as an art therapist, which led me out of the solitude of the studio toward a more engaged social practice. With clients, I saw over and over how creative work is healing and life affirming, helping people of different ages and backgrounds to become happier and build better relationships with their families and communities.

My current work with Swap-O-Rama-Rama (a community clothing swap and DIY wardrobe refashioning event) feels like art therapy on a broader level. People who attend these events come out with more than just some new clothes. They learn skills like sewing and knitting and needle felting; find resources within their neighborhoods; make new friends; and most important, step away from being passive consumers and move toward being creators!

Another project—the East Van Revolutionary Knitting Front, modeled after Grant Neufeld's Revolutionary Knitting Circle—was founded after a local school board trustee made a media splash when she appeared on the cover of the *National Firearms Journal* with her Colt .45 handgun. She was quoted as saying, "Some people knit. I like to shoot guns." She also advocated that women should be able to carry concealed weapons for safety reasons.

Now I don't believe that carrying a gun makes anyone safer. But I do know that knitting in public can start conversations and prompt smiles from strangers. I even once had a woman sitting next to me on the train give me a kiss on the cheek, saying it made her happy to see me knitting.

The East Van Revolutionary Knitting Front is intended to provide a relaxed, supportive place to meet and share skills, with a special invitation to community activists who may need to recharge their batteries and connect with each other informally. We also instigate public knitting actions as opportunities present themselves.

Survivors

Of course, there are other groups in your community that you can work with too. One that may not be obvious is survivors. The term *survivors* can be applied to a giant range of things from refugees to victims of domestic violence to cancer survivors, and groups that cater to these individuals are present, though often not readily visible, in every community. Get involved by donating an item for a charity raffle, with the proceeds benefiting a specific cause, or by organizing a drive for handmade items. Just start fighting for what you want to change through positive actions.

Homeless Animals

While you can't teach cats to knit or crochet, you can give the animals at the local pound a more pleasant environment by knitting blankets for them to lie on while they're waiting to be adopted. They can benefit from the tactile stimulation, and since animals are often considered part of the family, why not part of the community too?

Many different groups of people are unfortunately swept away from the hustle and bustle of the nine-to-five world and kept entirely separate. If working with these overlooked individuals seems like something you might enjoy, try contacting your local volunteering office or doing an online search for charitable groups in your area. Sometimes just spending a little time acknowledging someone's abilities, humanity, and goodness can make a bigger difference than you may ever know. And when handcrafts are involved, your kindness extends both inward and outward—in short, everybody wins.

Community Activism

Aiding others in your community in whatever way you choose is a form of activism. It speaks to things you'd like to change by helping to either promote a cause or improve a negative situation—a kind of positive activism unlike the common image of fist-waving protesters. Activism can be quiet and happy and joyful; it can fight without anger; and it can benefit everyone involved.

When you look at craft on a community level, it really can begin to chip away the veil that exists between you and your environment. By taking interest in your local community, you help yourself, your neighbors, the kids across town, and the town itself grow. How you choose to engage with others depends on you, since there is undoubtedly some sort of cause, sport, skill, or hobby that interests you and can be either practiced, improved, or taught. Sometimes it's not so easy to get off the couch, but as we all know, the hardest part is just standing up. Once you're on your feet? Piece of cake.

The most important thing is to help foster community interaction, however small, whether that means knitting with the elderly in a nursing home or leaving a scarf on a park bench with a note that says, "Take me home." It's about making your community *truly* yours and bringing love and thought into your daily surroundings.

| Connect with a Cause |

Make a list of causes you care for greatly. What's most important? Think about the range of groups that may need your help.
Chances are, whatever your interest, there's a group. Not sure
what causes you care about? Try thinking about what stories
you gravitate toward when you pick up the newspaper. We auto-
matically tend to read first about what we identify with, so this is
definitely a good starting point. Although your list may seem un-
wieldy at first, once you've gotten everything down on paper, try
whittling it down to a couple of causes that you consider impera-
tive. You can always expand your list or involvement later.

| Baby Steps to Getting Involved |

Once you've identified a cause you'd like to support, use the Internet, the phone book, or your own social circle to find an organization or group in your community. Check their websites to see
if there is a list of needed items for donation. Call and ask how you
can volunteer your time. Be aware that you may have an idea or
suggestion about how to help that they haven't thought of. Actually taking a step toward involvement can help you realize that
the hardest part is getting started. Concrete action takes you one
step away from thought and closer to involvement.

Dog Basket/Blanket

Designed by Naomi Johnstone

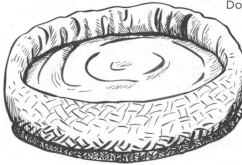

Dogs need a little extra coziness, too. This round bed offers comfort and a sense of safety for animals who need a little TLC.

| FINISHED MEASUREMENTS |

30" diameter and 4" high

| YARN |

Sirdar Country Style (45% acrylic/40% nylon/15% wool; 348 yards/100 grams): 4 balls #0502 Gemini Tweed

| NEEDLES |

One 36" or longer circular needle size US 5 (3.75 mm)
   One set double pointed needles (dpns) size US 5 (3.75 mm)
   Change needle size if necessary to obtain correct gauge.

| NOTIONS |

Stitch markers, iron-on interfacing in a strip approximately 4" x 2 1/2 yards, batting in a strip approximately 4" x 2 1/2 yards

| GAUGE |

20 sts and 28 rows = 4" (10 cm) in Stockinette stitch (St st)

| CABLE PATTERN |

C4B: Sl 2 sts to dpn, hold at the back of the work, k 2 sts from the left-hand needle, k 2 sts from dpn.
   C4F: Sl 2 sts to dpn, hold in the

front of the work, k 2 sts from the left-hand needle, k 2 sts from dpn.

| BLANKET |

With circular needle, CO 438 sts. *(Tip: Place marker after every 50 or 100 sts to help keep count; markers can be removed while knitting first rnd.)* Place marker and join being careful not to twist sts.

K all rnds for 4". P 1 rnd.

| CABLE BAND |

Work in cable pat for 4". P 1 rnd. K 2 rnds.

Continue as follows, changing to dpns when necessary:

Work in rnds for 1" as follows:
*K30, k2tog; rep from *.
K all rnds for 2".
**Work in rnds for 1" as follows:
K20, k2tog; rep from.
K all rnds for 2".

Rep from ** until you have 10" of knitting from the last purl row. Place marker.

***Work in rnds for 1" as follows:
*K10, k2tog; rep from *.
K all rnds for 2".
Rep from *** until piece measures 6" from marker.
*K5, k2tog; rep from * until 10 sts rem.

Cut yarn and thread yarn through sts.

| FINISHING |

Press work lightly on wrong side. Cut a strip of interfacing and a strip of batting 4" wide and long enough to go around the circumference of the blanket. Iron the interfacing to the wrong side of the facing. Place the batting against the interfacing and fold the facing under and sew the CO edge to the second purl rnd.

chapter six

---

knitting for a greater good

charitable knitting

IT'S NOT ABOUT WHO WRITES THE BIGGEST CHECK. IT'S
ABOUT WANTING TO HELP OTHERS FEEL SPECIAL, CARED FOR, OR SIM-
PLY WARM. THOSE OF US WHO KNIT CAN USE OUR NEEDLES AND YARN
stashes as a way of working toward change. If you sell your crafts, you can also
help charities by donating a certain percentage of the proceeds. Crafter Dayna
Mankowski, of craftyscientist.com, gives part of the profits from her craft sales
to charity instead of the actual items themselves. "When I worked for a large
corporation, I gave money to charity, but it was difficult to direct it to causes
that I wanted to donate to. Now I make items (cat toys and mats) that are sold
specifically for certain charities. So not only does money go to the charity, but
I get to make people (and their cats) happy with their purchases!"

Whether you donate some of your proceeds or crafted items themselves
doesn't matter; it's more about how you start viewing your creativity as a way
of giving back. Using creative energy to help the greater good helps to harness
the power you control with just your own two hands. By making items for both
yourself and your community, thus sharing your creativity with those around
you, you are embodying the positive change you want to see in the world.

Even if you don't have the time, interest, or ability to engage directly with the
community, knitting donations is still a great way to help them. This way, you
can give based on your own schedule and time available, as little or as much
as you want. You can choose the direction of what the item will look like. In
other words, it's a gentle way of easing yourself into donating to charity if
you're unsure, and a great way for you to give back to the community within
the limits of your hectic life.

When you start to explore charitable knitting, you will find that the
boundaries of how you can help continually expand. You can choose to aid

organizations in your city or people across the world. You can see the boundaries of your community expand and your impact on the world grow.

When you decide to help a charitable organization, there is no "wrong way" to go about it. The most important thing is that you do something! What you contribute varies mostly depending on what type of organization you're working with; the patterns in this book are just a starting point. Any number of toys can be created to give strength and hope and courage to both adults and children. You can make dramatic hats to cheer someone up or extralong socks to keep someone's knees warm. You can even customize a cozy for a daily accoutrement that could use a little spicing up.

When I started to really comprehend that by knitting for charity, I was knitting for an individual who needed a little extra comfort, joy or love, I began to grow as a knitter. My sense of compassion grew as well, because I started to think about what I would like if I were in a war zone or on the streets or living without some of life's most basic necessities. What would bring me comfort or help me dream or keep me fighting? The process allowed me to really see how little difference there was between me and the recipient of my work—we were just in different places or situations.

The History of Charitable Knitting

Although women knitted socks and donated clothing for soldiers in all the previous wars, perhaps the era best known for charitable knitting is the one encompassing World War II. During this time, pamphlets were produced by wool companies to promote their wool and offer patterns to knit for the troops, there were songs about knitting "for the boys," and women were encouraged to "knit their bit." The effort spent knitting for the war was so successful, it proved that something handmade could help those in need and was also a valid way to contribute to the community.

Pamphlets were distributed to inspire knitters to contribute and keep American soldiers overseas warm as they fought for justice; the text of these pamphlets was highly patriotic and assured crafters that they were "doing their part" by knitting for the troops. As noted in Anne Macdonald's *No Idle Hands*, quoting a World War II–era pamphlet from the wool company Bernat, claims such as "The Navy Department makes it official by voting this turtle-neck pullover the most wanted sweater by every mariner"; "[A]ctual war duties proved that abdominal belts kept many men out of the sick wards by protecting the body against sudden chills"; and "A knitted helmet is a must for every fighting man. He wears it in his plane, under his steel helmet, and to protect him against the cold on guard duty. He'll thank you many times over for your effort." The strangest part to me is that the yarn companies were publishing brochures on what to knit with their own wool, thus gaining a profit while encouraging women to knit more and more. Of course, the Red Cross also asked for knitters to donate items, but it realized no profit from such efforts. After the war ended, people still saw causes to knit for, but they were in a more private arena.

Now given the fact that times have changed and everything can be made so quickly by machine, yarn companies no longer publish brochures to encourage wartime knitting. I think this extraction of the commercial element from charitable knitting helps to ensure that no one feels pressured into making something they don't want to make; that's the beauty of charitable knitting—it's all about the personal choice of what you make for whom.

There is no fever pitch broadcasting on how we need to join the war effort now, but there is support if you decide to create something handmade for a cause, whether it is the military or something else. Although drives were held and charities arranged before the Internet, its instant access to information now allows word to be spread farther and wider to more people who may want to help. The idea that making something for someone else can possibly better both our and their existence has gained traction.

Choosing a Cause

There are so many charitable causes out there to contribute to, and since thousands of resources list charitable organizations, I won't go into specifics here. When selecting an organization to support, the most important thing is to find a cause that resonates with you personally and will then give your knitting more meaning. It doesn't matter if everyone you know is intent on knitting for one particular cause and you've decided to venture out on your own. Go for it! Take the time to consider what causes mean the most to you. Make a list of situations or illnesses that have affected your loved ones or social issues that have really been bothering you.

Once you've settled on what group you'd most like to support, think about how your craft could benefit those affected. Newborns need little hats to keep their heads warm. People who don't feel good like something cozy to wrap up in. The cement floors in animal shelters are much more comfortable when there's a handmade blanket to snuggle up on. It's all about finding a need and then seeing how you can fulfill it.

If you already have a group in mind, contact its head office or local chapter office directly and see if there is a way you can help via craft. Most groups have either a need that requires a solution or a list of things they need donated. Season and climate may factor here too, as there is less need for winter scarves for the homeless in Miami than there is in Chicago.

Maybe it was a coincidence, but during my first (and only) winter in New York City, I learned both how to knit and how to appreciate scarves. I learned new ways to wear them and fully realized the comfort they can bring on an extra chilly, windy day. After a winter of being comforted by these accessories and subsequent months of continuously knitting them, I was intrigued when one of the women I knew from an online craft forum started by Jean Railta (getcrafty.com) wrote that a local shelter for battered women was collecting scarves to give to its residents. Presented with the opportunity to craft at home on my own time between work and school and other activities, I signed up to donate several scarves. Aside from the deadline for completion, the color and design were completely in my control, and I liked that.

A few evenings a week, I would work on these scarves, surprised at how I found myself taking more care in their construction than I had even for scarves I'd made for my loved ones. It seemed that these scarves needed to be extra special because they were going to women who were in need of something beautiful. I was painstakingly careful, wanting them to be perfect, and I enjoyed thinking about how they would be worn by the shelter's residents.

When I was done, I carefully wrote and attached cards with instructions on how to care for them, making sure my handwriting was pretty. After I had sent them off, I came home and started yet another scarf. Upon its completion, I wondered why I was so taken with this project, as I had made dozens of scarves before. I think it has something to do with the fact that when we give someone we know and love a personal gift, it's most often at a time of celebration—a graduation, a birthday, a holiday. These gifts are given as acts of joy and may end up in a closet with other similar gifts, maybe never seeing the light of day. In making the scarves for the shelter, I was taking the personal part of the equation out, as well as the calendar-based one. I was making something for someone who could really use it. I wasn't doing this to give myself a pat on the back or atone for any misdeeds, but for the love of creating something new and for humanity. Need plus love equals beautifully crafted results.

Charity knitting gives us a chance to try a new project or test a different technique, to use some of our stash, to team up with friends, to help a cause we care about, to provide strength and love to others, to fight helplessness, and to comfort strangers. Perhaps you'll discover even more wonderful benefits when you start donating your handmade creations to those in need.

Faythe Levine

FAYTHE LEVINE LIVES IN MILWAUKEE, WISCONSIN WHERE SHE IS THE CO-OWNER OF THE BRICK AND MORTAR SPACE PAPER BOAT BOUTIQUE AND GALLERY AND COORDINATES ART VS. CRAFT, THE LOCAL INDIE CRAFT FAIR. SHE IS ALSO THE DIRECTOR AND COAUTHOR OF *HANDMADE NATION,* A BOOK AND DOCUMENTARY FILM ABOUT THE INDIE CRAFT MOVEMENT. IN HER SPARE TIME SHE STILL MANAGES TO MAKE CRAFTS EVERY ONCE AND A WHILE.

By 2002, I was living in Milwaukee and opened Flying Fish Gallery. The small gallery space featured local artists and had a tiny space where we sold handmade work from around the country. I was still making things, and I knew others who were making things, but I wasn't tapped into other outlets to sell my work, when I heard about a craft fair in Chicago called Renegade. It was for younger artists, crafters, and designers, people who made "edgy, nontraditional" items. I applied to be a vendor with no experience selling my work in a public environment and was accepted as a participant. I put together a bunch of work, including handbags, accessories, and postcards, and sold under my gallery name Flying Fish. That was the beginning of my romance with indie craft.

When I arrived at the event, I immediately noticed that other participants embraced the DIY ethics of my teen years. There were emerging artists who were creating an independent economy, free from corporate ties, similar to my music scene. It was all about stressing the importance of artist-made goods and setting itself apart from mass-produced junk. All around me were techniques of traditional handiwork mixed with modern aesthetics, politics, punk, feminism, and art. Everyone there had their own agendas, but with the common thread of being makers.

I left the show filled with a sense of empowerment. I wanted to make a living selling handmade items and art, and I felt like I now had a platform from which to do so. Since I had little experience with the retail/wholesale market and no real idea about getting my work out there, I tapped into the online community that was beginning to form around indie craft. Websites like www.craftster.org and theswitchboards.com made me feel like anything I set my mind to was possible. I participated in online forums about topics like starting an online business, where to print business cards, how to approach shops, how to price your goods, and so on. Many of the people I met through those forums are now good friends across the country. It has been so amazing to see everyone figure out their niche and make it work.

Flying Fish Design started with a small line of products that included my most popular seller, the Messenger Owl. This was a felt plush owl with a pocket on the back to tuck a note into. Each owl had ten hand-cut pieces that were sewn together on the same sewing machine my mom had taught me to sew on (I still use it) and stuffed. After receiving a few wholesale orders for 100+ of the same item, I started to rethink my way of ordering supplies and streamlined my process to make it easier on my pocketbook and body. Hand cutting thousands of pattern pieces really takes its toll on your wrists and hands.

I made a lot of mistakes along the way, but I also made a lot of friends and learned how to start a business on my own terms. I also realized, after working very hard at Flying Fish for three years, that what I really wanted to do was help promote other people's work and focus on my brick-and-mortar shop, Paper Boat Boutique & Gallery, as well as the craft fair in Milwaukee I started called Art vs. Craft. I know I will always have the creative drive within me to want to make new stuff, but I have learned that I don't want to make the same thing thousands of times. At least I know that now, and I wouldn't trade my learning process for anything.

I see what is going on now within the craft community, and I am so proud to be a part of such a supportive, growing group that is based on creativity and self-motivation. I know this community will survive and sustain. Whether you just want to create for the sake of making or to start your own business, there is an accessible network at your fingertips waiting to offer help and experience.

Creating Solidarity for a Cause

Knitting circles are not just places to compare and contrast knitting techniques; when they meet in support of a cause, they can be small circles of peace that provide a bit of positive energy to a negative situation. When we gather with other like-minded individuals in support of a cause, we can share our concerns and come up with solutions together.

When our communities, cities, and nations are under stress, it's hard not to wear a shell of either defiance or denial. Day after day of the same bad news that never seems to end can take its toll on us, even though we may think we're handling the situation just fine. Personally, I can begin to gauge how I'm feeling when I turn on the news or listen to talk radio. Some days I turn it up and listen intently, whereas other days, I either tune it out or turn it off. Sometimes there is so much sadness to take in that it simply gets overwhelming. Having close knitting circles that we can turn to is one way to build a support network. We can also view charity organizations as extensions of our knitting circle. When we identify with a group that is trying to make a difference, even if it is an organization outside of our immediate area, we can start to feel less alone and helpless in our desire to create positive change.

Afghans for Afghans is a well-known organization that gathers warm items for children in Afghanistan. By supporting their cause, I see myself making a statement against the war by knitting vests or hats for children who are affected by the current conflict in that country. I not only disseminate my feelings when people ask what I'm making, but by adding to the number of donations, I know that I am not alone. I'm not going to say that I've done my share to help the world by making a few things here and there, but I know that just by being aware of what's happening and doing *something*, I am not sitting quietly and okaying things.

Whenever I send donations out to a charity, I tend to ask around among others who knit to see if anyone wants to donate with me. Without pushing, I note when I'll be sending the donations out and collect from whoever wants to participate. When I send out that package with all of our donations in it, it helps me feel less separate from the rest of the world. I think that's really the root of any hobby or pastime—making that connection to a part of you that resonates with both yourself and others. One of the reasons I became interested in knitting to begin with was because it was a portable, versatile craft with a worldwide history that didn't have a steep learning curve. I guess, in a way, you could say I'm learning more about the subculture of knitting, about the ways unrelated people connect through a common interest. I think that's important, because not only does it allow you to connect, it also allows you to keep learning.

On those days when I turn off the television or the radio because there seem to be too many problems and horrors to process, knowing that there is something I can do, however small, to make someone else's life easier alleviates some of those feelings of helplessness. I like the fact that I, as one person, can do something for one other person and then another and then another. It condenses the world's problems to a scale that I can relate to and helps make everything feel a little less out of control, even though the media are still going to report horror after horror.

Knitting for charities encourages us to think outside of our own circle of family and friends. As the days add up, so does our knowledge about certain causes, as well as the number of things we have donated. In remembering that we don't exist in a vacuum, we can feel more connected to people far away from where we live. I know that somewhere, in places like Bulgaria and Norway, there is someone sitting and knitting just like me, that someone in Afghanistan is wearing something I made, and in a way—just for a moment— the world doesn't seem so gigantic. I'm not trying to escape from computers or technology; I'm trying to remember what it's like to understand that the world is much larger than my immediate environment, yet not so overwhelming that I can't feel a part of it.

Donna Druchunas

DONNA DRUCHUNAS IS THE AUTHOR OF FOUR KNITTING BOOKS. SHE ALSO WRITES ABOUT CHARITY AND ACTIVIST KNITTING AT SUBVERSIVEKNITTING.COM.

My grandmother knitted because she enjoyed feeling the yarn in her fingers as she formed stitches with her needles and because she loved to wrap her children and grandchildren in handmade sweaters and afghans to surround us with soft reminders of her love. From time to time, friends would ask her to knit for money or in exchange for other goods, but she never took on the task. Her stitching was for herself and her family, an act of love and belonging.

When I started knitting more than a decade ago, I thought I would follow Grandma's tradition by knitting for myself and my family. Not having children or grandchildren, however, meant that my family was quite a bit smaller than hers. I loved making the stitches and feeling the fiber in my hands, but simply filling my closets with lovely sweaters and accessories didn't feel fulfilling to me.

I've since found satisfaction in using knitting to explore political and social issues in several ways. All knitting, especially making projects with hand-spun or organic yarns, makes a statement against the consumerism that is rampant in Western society. Even when I am knitting something for myself, by creating something from scratch, something uniquely mine, I defy the standards of mass production and conformity that we are bombarded with in the media. Giving handmade gifts for birthdays and holidays provides a way to share these values with others.

Knitting for charity allows me to spread the warmth and love that is captured in each knitted piece to others outside my immediate family. Offering free charity knitting patterns on my website allows me to encourage others to do the same and to write about how knitting relates to social and political issues that concern me. Reaching out to others, with stitches and words, is my attempt to spread compassion and joy and to help make the world a better place one person—and one stitch—at a time.

Knitting unusual pieces that carry a visual message, in addition to the messages intrinsic to being handmade, allows me to speak more directly about my passions and the social issues that are on my mind. Because these items are not meant to be reproduced by others, I find freedom in creativity that is not always present when I have to write a pattern for publication.

I plan to explore all of these ideas further in the future and to work on knitted art pieces that convey political and social messages. Because politics touches every aspect of our lives and I believe that the personal *is* political, I feel like I am following in my grandmother's footsteps, even though our goals may seem different to the casual observer.

The Secondary Benefits of Charity Knitting

Beyond making items for individuals or as donations, charity knitting has a number of "secondary" benefits that you might find unexpected. One of the best things about finding the pleasing aspects to your work is that it fuels you to create more! The benefits listed here are by no means comprehensive; feel free to add your own.

Getting Rid of Your Stash

Crafters tend to accumulate a lot of stuff. Bits and bobs of thread, needles, yarn, string, buttons, anything that may come in handy for a future creation. I've met few crafters who didn't have a room or a closet or a drawer full of things they had acquired along the way, either by purchase or gift or the purging of another crafter's stash. Knitting for charity is a great way to bust that stash because you can make a variety of things, like hats, scarves, and mittens, that take less than a whole skein.

Trying Something New

If you've ever wanted to try a new technique, knitting something that pushes your skills and will be given to someone else ups the ante. Instead of knowing that you can hide those seams later, you know that once you've given this item away, it will actually be used; therefore, it will need to be as strong and well made as it can possibly be.

Teaming Up with Friends

Many charities call for blankets, which can easily be done as a group project. This can also serve as a stash buster as knitters use leftover bits to make squares.

Finding Closure

In chapter 3, I talked about knitting after my grandfather died of cancer. I was living on a farm in England when he died, and although I had seen him a few months prior to his death, I never got to say a proper good-bye. I made it back for the funeral, but I was still upset at the loss and needed a way to process my grief. I ended up making a cap for a chemotherapy patient that he himself might have worn, and I knitted bravery and strength into every stitch. The hours I worked on that cap I spent having happy memories of him and his good, strong qualities. Of course when I was done, I was still terribly sad, but through knitting, I had processed his loss and reminded myself of all the good times.

Working with the Stitch

Sometimes people want to do something for charity, but as they can't commit to a regular time to volunteer are at a loss for how they can contribute. Often when people start thinking about making something for charity, they worry about not being talented enough ("Why would anyone want to wear my ill-knitted hat?"). But what they forget is that they can work on their knitting techniques as they go along. Just because the first row you knit has lots of holes doesn't mean you can't unstitch it and start over. You're on your own deadline and are in control of what you ultimately donate, so what do you have to lose?

Providing Strength and Love

Although not all charities focus on helping those who are less fortunate, many of them do. If you believe that things such as positivity really do go into what you knit, you can choose to knit love or strength or wisdom or health or anything you wish into each garment. In your own quiet way, you can bestow strength on others in your community by using your hands and some yarn.

There are many reasons for you to consider donating handmade items to charity. Ultimately, what you are doing is bringing some comfort, beauty, and joy into the lives of others, honoring them and their spirit by making something that you yourself would cherish. Different projects call for different types of yarn or different types of garments, but that doesn't mean you shouldn't have pride in whatever you send.

There may very well be a day when you're making something for your favorite charity and someone asks what you're doing; when you tell them, they want to know why. Somehow I don't think anyone would ever ask why you're knitting a sweater for your mother or father; why should making something for someone in need be any more difficult to understand? As human beings we have a need for warmth and comfort, and by using our skills at craft, we can help provide both.

Knitting for Good Actions

| Collect Donations |

Pick a charity that needs donations and ask your friends to help make items to give. Estimate how many items you think you'll receive, and call the charity organizers to make sure they don't have enough already (sometimes certain charities can be inundated with things, while others are lacking). Set a date for collection, and if your friends don't know quite what to knit, provide a pattern for guidance. Even better, designate an evening for you all to work together on the items to be donated.

| Spare a Square |

Perhaps you're not ready to make something for charity on your own. What about making an afghan with a bunch of friends? First, decide how large you would like the blanket to be, which will largely depend on the type of charity it will be going to. Then use the approximate size to break the afghan down into individual squares. For example, a small lap afghan is 24 x 36 inches. Both numbers are divisible by six, which makes it easy to divide into 6-inch squares; four squares across and six squares down are needed to make the afghan. Put out the word to those you know that you're collecting squares (note size and color, if appropriate). Once you've collected all the squares you need and stitched them together, you've gotten not only your community involved in charitable knitting, but yourself as well.

Oatlion

Designed by Katie Aaberg

Sometimes you may want to knit a toy, rather than an item of clothing, for a child. Given the scary situations that children can sometimes be put in or are witness to, this toy lion knitted by Katie Aaberg reminds them to be strong and brave.

| FINISHED MEASUREMENTS |

7" long x 6" tall

| YARN |

Brown Sheep Company Cotton Fleece (80% cotton/20% wool; 215 yards/100 grams): 1 skein each #CW310 Wild Orange (A) and #CW100 Cotton Ball (B) (you will use less than 150 yards of each color); small amounts of #CW201 Barn Red (C) and #CW145 Black Forest (D).

| NEEDLES |

One 36" circular (circ) needle size US 3 (3.25 mm)

One set double pointed needles (dpns) size US 3 (3.25 mm)

Change needle size if necessary to obtain correct gauge.

| NOTIONS |

Crochet hook size D, stitch markers, tapestry needle, washable stuffing, white glue (optional)

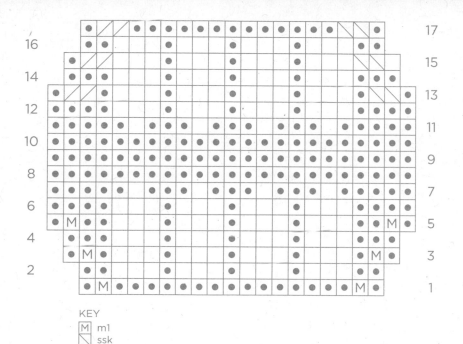

KEY

M	m1
⟋	ssk
⟍	k2tog
●	black, k on RS, p on WS
□	white, k on RS, p on WS

| GAUGE |

28 sts and 36 rows = 4″ (10 cm) in Stockinette Stitch (St st)

| BUTT (MAKE 1) |

With B and dpns, CO 72 sts, divide evenly onto 3 needles—24 sts each needle. Join being careful not to twist sts and k 17 rnds.

Next rnd: [K8, place marker (M)] 9 times.

Next rnd: [K to 2 sts before M, k2tog, sl M] 9 times—9 sts decreased.

Next rnd: K. Rep last 2 rows a total of 6 times—18 sts rem.

Next rnd: K2tog around—9 sts rem. Cut yarn leaving long end, thread through sts and pull tight to close. Pull end down through center and secure on inside.

| LEGS (MAKE 4) |

Note: When changing colors, use jogless jog (see Abbreviations and Terms on page 146).

With B and dpns, CO 24 sts,

divide evenly onto 3 needles—8 sts each needle.

Join being careful not to twist sts and k 6 rnds.

With A, k 6 rnds.

With B, k 6 rnds. Rearrange sts so that there are 9 sts on needle 1, 7 sts on needle 2, and 8 sts on needle 3.

Next rnd: [K1, k2tog] around—16 sts rem. K 2 rnds, then rearrange sts so that there are 6 sts on needle 1, 4 sts on needle 2, and 6 sts on needle 3. Next rnd: K2tog around—8sts rem. Break yarn leaving long end, thread through sts, and pull tight to close. Pull yarn end down through center and secure on inside.

| HEAD (MAKE 1) |

Mane: With A and circ, CO 285 sts. Working back and forth, work as follows:

Row 1: K1, *k2, sl first st over 2nd st on right-hand needle; rep from *—143 sts.

Row 2: P1, [p2tog] across—72 sts.

Row 3: Knit.

Transfer to dpns, dividing sts evenly over 3 needles—24 sts each needle.

Join being careful not to twist sts and k 5 rnds.

Rnd 6: Needle 1: K24; needle 2: K1, M1, k to last st, M1, k1; needle 3: K24—2 sts increased.

Rnd 7: Knit.

Rep rnds 6 and 7 a total of 8 times. Rep rnd 6 once more—90 sts.

Rearrange sts evenly over 3 needles—30 sts each needle. K 7 rnds.

Rnd 8: [K10, place M] 9 times.

Rnd 9: [K to 2 sts before M, k2tog, sl M] 9 times—9 sts decreased.

Rnd 10: Knit.

Rep rnds 9 and 10 a total of 8 times—18 sts rem.

Next rnd: K2tog around—9 sts rem.

Break yarn leaving long end, thread through sts and pull tight to close.

Pull yarn end down through center and secure on inside.

| MOUTH (MAKE 1) |

Note: Work back and forth using two dpns.

Teeth: With D and dpn, CO 17 sts. P 1 row. Starting with a k row, work 17 rows of chart in St st. P 1 row. Bind off.

Lips: With C, CO 8 sts. Work in St st for 8". Bind off. Sew ends together. With right sides facing, sew one edge of lips around teeth panel, covering edges of teeth.

| EARS (MAKE 2) |

With A, CO 12 sts and divide evenly over 3 dpns—4 sts each needle. K 4 rnds.

Rearrange sts so there are 3 sts on needle 1, 6 sts on needle 2, and 3 sts on needle 3.

Rnd 1: Needle 1: K1, k2tog; needle 2: Ssk, k2, k2tog; needle 3: Ssk, k1—8 sts rem

Rnd 2: Knit.

Rnd 3: Needle 1: K2tog; needle 2: Ssk, k2tog; needle 3: Ssk—4 sts rem.

Break yarn leaving long end, thread through sts and pull tight to close. Pull yarn end down through center of ear, creating rounded top.

| TAIL (MAKE 1) |

With crochet hook and holding two strands of A together, make slip knot 8" from end and ch10. Make one more chain, drawing loop through until it is 2" long. Cut yarn leaving 2" at the end. Tie end and loop together with overhand knot. Optional: Add a drop of glue to knot. Cut loop and trim ends.

| FINISHING |

Position mouth over the closed end of the head. With D, sew the black part of the mouth down flat to the face along the inside edge of the lips; tack it down in the center as well. With C, sew the outside edge of the lips to the face, lightly stuffing the lips as you go. With D, embroider circular eyes on the face. With B, embroider the highlights on the eyes. Sew the ears onto the head using the CO tails. Stuff head and butt pieces firmly. Sew the open end of the butt to the head, stitching them together under the ruffled mane; stuff the body firmly before closing completely. Using the CO tail, sew the 3-row opening in the mane closed. Stuff the legs firmly, and sew them onto the body, 2 behind the mane and 2 in front of it, placing the back legs 2" apart and the front legs 1" apart so that the Oatlion can sit. Using the unchained end, sew the tail into place on the butt.

part three  knitting *for* the world

chapter seven

making statements about the way we live

KNITTING MEANS DIFFERENT THINGS TO DIFFERENT PEOPLE. FOR SOME, IT IS SIMPLY A RELAXING AND PRODUCTIVE HOBBY. FOR OTHERS, IT MAY BE ANY OR ALL OF THE FOLLOWING: A WAY OF EXPRESSING LOVE AND GRATitude to a friend, a way of supporting individuals in need, a way of lessening the environmental impact of mass-produced goods, a way of protesting sweatshop labor, a way to make a livelihood, or a way of supplying needed household items.. Whatever our reason for knitting, through the craft itself, we constantly have the opportunity to make profound statements about the ways in which we live.

Supporting Handmade

I believe that the personal is political and that every choice and action we make affects not only ourselves and our lives, but the lives of others as well. Handmade brings life back to a level where connection with others is possible. By knowing that a single person, rather than a machine, has made something unique injects the personal into more aspects of daily existence. It isn't difficult to move toward homemade. For example, I recently decided to buy a new food dish for my cat because she had the habit of flipping her bowl over incessantly. Knowing what the larger pet chains had to offer, I ventured into my local pet store one afternoon to see if I could find a bowl that was more suited to my special cat.

On a shelf near the register was a display of handmade ceramic food and water dishes of different sizes and shapes and colors. I picked them up and found them instantly heavier than the one I had, thanks to the type of clay that had been used. Before I left, I noticed that the dishes were made by a self-employed local artisan. I bought two new bowls, one for food and the other for water. Once I was home, I replaced the old dishes with the newer heavier ones and was surprised at how they instantly made that corner of the room look more lived in and more like "home." The unique curve of the bowls, along with their individual glazes, made the room look less antiseptic than the steel ones I had been using. Even the way they sounded when my cat scooted them around the floor was more organic, an added joy given the fact that they were also too heavy for her to tip.

While this may seem like a silly example, it was just one of my many everyday decisions, and I made this particular one because I happened to stop in my small, local pet store instead of a larger one with perhaps more choices. You don't have to make huge changes in your life to bring the handmade into it, you just need to be open to the idea that bringing the handmade into your life may change it, in the tiniest of ways, for the better.

One of the biggest benefits to the resurgence of handmade is the creation of a stronger microeconomy, both in the United States and beyond. Due to our over-reliance on mass-produced goods, we have started to look at where our products come from instead of merely seeing them, wanting them, and buying them without thought. Rachel Hospodar, a crafter from San Francisco, sees craft as a form of passive resistance: "I think the handcraft movement is a hopeful sign of a deeper rejection of modern society's factory-driven lifestyle. Rapidly escalating environmental and human rights concerns are showing people how poisonous the mass-manufactured lifestyle is, and they are seeking alternatives."

The triple occurrence of an increased interest in the origins of different goods, the quest for originality, and greater global awareness has given individuals all over the world a better chance to have their goods exported and sold for a fair price instead of a pittance. This new attitude shows not only a greater curiosity about the world outside of our individual bubbles, but also that our attention is turning (even if only slightly) away from the megamarts, super-stores, and easy, instant everything.

At the most basic level, there are two ways of keeping the handmade market successful: by buying items handmade by others, and by selling our own handmade items. Both are valuable ways of developing and supporting a microeconomy that has a direct benefit for the individual, rather than less personal corporations, here and abroad.

Today with the craft resurgence in full bloom, websites such as Etsy.com, which provides a place to sell your wares online, and craft fairs such as the Bazaar Bizarre and the Renegade Craft Fair offer the possibility that one day we might be able to quit our day jobs and craft full-time. For some, the making and selling of crafts has made self-employment a viable option. But for many others, the hope of one day being able to quit their day jobs and become full-time makers remains a goal for the future as they work various gigs to pay the bills and craft in their spare time.

You don't have to peddle your handmade creations to participate positively in handmade microeconomies. When you buy handmade, the craft network gets stronger, the demand for handmade products becomes greater, and hopefully we send a message about the negative effects of mass-manufactured goods. By putting our hard-earned money toward something we believe in, we're doing more than just acquiring a nice, new item—we're supporting an individual and helping someone grow his or her business and work toward becoming self-sufficient. By supporting individuals who are working for themselves, we are circumventing big business by creating a system that sustains our peers and people whose work we like. By purchasing things directly from the makers, we are ensuring that they get the full cost that they deserve for those items without any commission held back. We are helping them move toward their dreams and not a large company's bottom line.

The fact that there is a network of literally thousands of self-employed crafty individuals in the United States alone speaks to not only good timing and creativity, but also to the way a smaller economy can exist outside of the mainstream—in this case, largely aided by craft fairs and the Internet.

Valerie Soles

VALERIE SOLES LIVES IN BROOKLYN AND SELLS HER PRETTY HANDMADE CLOTHES ON DEARBIRTHDAY.COM.

The process by which I arrived at the decision to sell the things I make was so natural and gradual that it hardly seemed to have involved any actual decision making at all. There is definitely a compulsive element to my personality, an inability to keep my fidgety hands still. I've always made things and would, in fact, get in trouble at various day jobs for losing track of my assigned tasks while preoccupied with little side projects. The more I made, the more I started to think about the act of making itself—the process, the time involved, the effort expended, and so on. Examining pieces I had created, I would compare them to similar store-bought pieces and wonder, naturally, how I could afford to buy a pair of jeans or a sweater somewhat regularly with my modest salary. I realized that if I were making such things and selling them, I would not be able to support myself if I charged prices that were competitive with those of the retail chains. What had started out as a very natural, unexamined activity, became for me an exploration of ethics and personal politics as well. After a little research into the sordid practices involved in bringing me the various items and products I use every day, it seemed only natural to try to distance myself from that.

It often sounds excessively lofty or preachy when makers start extolling the virtues of self-sufficiency through making. It can be a difficult subject to broach; as with most topics that suggest the importance of a lifestyle change, it is hard to make the point without alienating your peers. But it shouldn't be that way at all; in fact, the opposite should be true. The greatest thing about crafting or making or whatever you want to call it is that it is by its very nature an inclusive act; it's empowering to know that with patience, determination, and a little research, anyone can make just about anything she needs. Not only are you bucking the system when you do so, but it's a powerful self-affirmation and just a really big nerdy thrill!

At the same time, it's unrealistic to expect that most people these days have the time to make all of their own things, which is why it's so amazingly wonderful that there are so many options for buying handmade or ethically produced necessities. I think I've been very lucky that my inquiry and exploration into the handmade versus the mass-produced market has coincided with an increased public awareness and appreciation for the same ethical concerns that brought me here. I've found that, although I have to charge more for a dress than most retail stores do, customers have a better understanding of where their money is going, and most of them just love the fact that their dress was handmade—it just feels more special.

Supporting Global Microeconomies

Once you start thinking about how microeconomies are supporting your peers and your local community, it's a not-so-giant leap to microeconomies on the global level. While community and global microeconomies differ in many ways, both have the same goal—to provide income and a sense of economic stability for those who rely on their own skills and savvy to survive.

Microeconomies help mothers (who can keep their children within arm's reach instead of across town) turn their kitchen tabletop operations into successful ventures that pay the bills. They also help individuals in poverty-stricken areas where jobs are scarce provide for their families without resorting to working in sweatshops, relocating across borders, breaking the law, or simply going without. The power of the microeconomy is that producers make a wage that is satisfactory to them and of their own devising, instead of relying on someone else to decide how much their time is worth, and they can make a more livable wage. Giving producers a say in what they earn breeds a sense of pride and self-worth instead of hopeless feelings about a desperate economic situation. With greater job satisfaction comes harder work, which means a greater and more diverse production of goods, which pushes makers to put in their best creative efforts.

Microeconomies are all about individuals striving to make their living conditions better for themselves and their loved ones. When we discover that people are making products from their own sweat and tears, we can feel much better supporting them and their work, rather than fueling some mass-market business. In countries plagued by hunger, drought, weather-related disasters, and war, these microeconomies can slowly help rebuild lives in ways that factory jobs never can. In places where people's spirits have been robbed by injustice, being given the opportunity to work on something of their own choice can mean the world, whether it is through a grant or a gift from an organization or a charity. By simply gaining an awareness of where our products come from, we can create significant change in other people's lives.

The Meaning of Handmade

What does the rise of the microeconomy mean to us, the makers and crafters? Microeconomies help show those of us who wish to live off of our creative efforts that we can be simultaneously autonomous and actively involved with our own growth. This is especially important in countries where personal freedom—which so many of us take for granted—is new or still on the horizon. For individuals in these countries, being allowed the chance to help themselves, their communities, and their nation grow brings a little less worry about the future as they realize they have a possible way out and a way forward.

In the larger scheme of things, the rise in interest in crafts may not seem like much. But crafters are showing by example how people the world over can hopefully one day help themselves by using resources like the Internet to earn income. As we watch people become successful ethically and on their own terms, we grow stronger as individuals, as citizens, and as human beings. Each time people provide for themselves and their families based on work they have done themselves (and not for anyone else), the network of micro-economies gets stronger and individuals' voices get louder.

The crux of the microeconomy is the personal aspect. As small networks of crafters help support one another to keep their own businesses afloat, and as these acts of choice gain momentum, the hope is that ever-more consumers will see the value of alternative economies. Given the ethical nature that is often associated with it, supporting an economy outside of mass production is only a few steps away from creating for charitable causes. And it is in this continuous connection to individuals and creative growth that craft's healing powers shine the brightest, thanks to the way it allows us to interact with others both directly and indirectly.

Cat Mazza

CAT MAZZA IS AN ARTIST LIVING IN TROY, NEW YORK. LEARN MORE ABOUT HER WORK AT MICROREVOLT.ORG.

Craft on its own is not radical or a form of activism or a political act. For the work that I do with microRevolt the question is "What is the political potential of craft?" Artists, entrepreneurs, and activists have recently used craft (not for the first time in history) as a medium to engage. Since craft lends itself to hobbyist groups that meet regularly and have rotating members, it can be a way of circulating ideas as well as providing a common space for dialogue and exchange. Though "craftivism" seems to be associated with left-of-center politics, various agendas and messages have manifested through craft. For example, whereas in 2005 pro-choice activists planned to litter the steps of the Supreme Court with knitted wombs to protest the Court's conservative bent, antiabortion activists crocheted gowns for unborn fetuses.

I came to love knitting as a reaction to working so intensely with technology and became inspired by it as a preindustrial skill. It helped me consider the wide gap between handcraft and manufacturing and got me interested in early industrial capitalism, the dawn of sweatshops, and the subsequent labor movement. The political force of this movement rose out of the labor exploitation by the clothing industry whose technology in many ways replaced handcraft. When considering this question of the political potential of craft, it isn't craft alone that is powerful, but the scope of the people who engage in it.

Considering Our Global Impact

When you live in a world where there's always food and water and shelter and clothes (not to mention movies and cars and MP3 players), it's hard to think of life in any other way. You turn on the tap, water comes out. You go to the gas station and fill up your tank. You walk through the grocery store and have your pick of literally thousands of foods, most of them only a microwave zap away. When there's no reason to doubt the perpetual existence of all this, there's no constant reminder of just how lucky we are.

But for millions of people, life is very much the opposite. Their children go hungry; they walk by example for miles to get water; they go to sleep to the sounds of gunfire and explosions. We all inhabit the same planet, even though it seems like some individuals come from somewhere completely and totally alien. When I was a child, I used to stare at the television footage about droughts and famines and have no real concept that the people experiencing those things were just like me. It seems silly now, decades later, but it seemed like a play or a movie where people played dress up and didn't really die of hunger or cold or thirst. When I got older, I wondered what I could do to help. I felt powerless in the face of so much pain and horror and tried to push away the harsh realities of others' lives by deadening my own emotions. Neither option was helpful, although I can say that childish innocence is much easier to forgive than apathy.

In 1999 when the Albanian refugees were fleeing Kosovo like a river, I was shocked to watch people literally carrying all their belongings on their backs as they left their homeland for somewhere new and relatively safer. The cameras would get so close that you could see every emotion on their faces, and the reporters tended to leave much of the drama to speak for itself, as a near-silent procession extended into the horizon. Apathy and childish innocence converged as I began to internalize the sheer number of people involved and how, given different circumstances, I could have been on the other side of the camera as someone far away watched me.

I carried those images with me when I started knitting items for charity. I took the moment where "that could be me" and started to make things, knowing that they would help one person at a time. Although it didn't always seem like "enough," I knew I was doing something toward relieving someone's cold bones somewhere. And I hoped that my scarves would wrap around them and convey, even if just a little bit, a sense of hope and love and kindness. Once I started thinking about things I could do on a more global level, I started finding groups that were using craft to elucidate problems of epidemic proportions.

As a way to subvert the traditional form of the petition, where it takes only a few seconds to sign your name, one knitting group started a project with the organization Wateraid to bring attention to the number of people who don't have regular access to clean drinking water or adequate toilets. The project, Knit a River, asked for donations of knitted six-by-six-inch blue squares that were used to form a "river" that visually showed both how large the problem was globally and how many people supported the campaign. Instead of collecting a mass of signed names in protest, the river was displayed at various festivals and events. It's easy to ignore a petition, but not so easy to ignore a massive sea of blue squares that blocks your path and leads you to wonder what its purpose is.

It is this asking of questions that is one of the most important aspects of helping raise awareness of needs or inequities across the globe. For me, it was the news, not understanding what could have happened to have caused thousands of people to flee their country with just a few (if any) possessions. It was an exodus, something I had never seen on such a scale before, happening right before my eyes, where I couldn't ignore it or stop myself from asking questions. Projects like Knit a River accomplish the same thing by making people curious and encouraging them to learn more.

Raising our sense of awareness not only helps us stay informed of world events, it also helps us better understand the specific role that we are to play in those events. What resources do we have? What ideas can we share? What can we give? By not alienating ourselves from our immediate surroundings, we gather compassion and empathy as well as understanding. We ask more questions, envision more ideas, and initiate conversations. We can do all of this and more, just by remaining present and open to the world around us.

Knitting for Good Actions

| Making Choices with Our Wallets |

Do you know where your money goes? On a notepad, jot down the last ten items you spent money on. Did you buy these items at big-box retailers or from a large-scale producer? Or did they come from more independent businesses? If your list contains mostly big-box retail names, is there anywhere else you can purchase the same items locally? If the list contains mostly independent businesses, was supporting them a conscious act of ethical consumerism or an act of geographic convenience?

| Getting Local—Even If Only for a Cup of Coffee |

I fully admit to drinking entirely too much corporate-chain coffee. I also fully admit to a full-blown coffee addiction. With a giant coffee store chain outlet (almost literally) on every corner, it's a pretty easy habit to keep up. But what about the little guys? Until I actually pried myself away from one certain giant chain, convinced that I was never going to be adequately caffeinated again, I started checking out the local coffee shops in my area. I was overjoyed to find such niceties as more comfy chairs, free wi-fi, and locally roasted coffee. Some of the shops even had cooler mugs and played music they liked instead of hawking CDs by the register. But it wasn't until I started looking for these places that they were truly on my radar.

Do you have some sort of habit that is currently fulfilled only by a chain or franchise? Try going to local places in your area, if only to experiment. See whether there are any surprises.

Manos Silk Blend Socks

Designed by Janice Bye

I had no idea of the joy of handmade socks until a few months ago, and my feet may never be the same! Socks keep our feet warm and dry and cozy, and when they're donated to charity, they can really make someone's day.

| SIZES |

Women's one size

| FINAL MEASUREMENTS |

6" x desired length

| YARN |

Manos Silk Blend (70% merino wool/30% silk; 150 yards/50 grams): 1 skein each #3117 Violets (color 1) and #3071 Wisteria (color 2).

| NEEDLES |

One set double pointed needles (dpns) size US 4 (3.5 mm)
 Change needle size if necessary to obtain correct gauge.

| NOTIONS |

Stitch marker

| GAUGE |

26 sts and 36 rows = 4" (10 cm) in Stockinette stitch (St st)

| NOTE |

First sock is worked with color 1 as A and color 2 as B. Second sock reverses colors.

| SOCKS |

With color A, CO 60 sts.
 Distribute sts as follows: 15 sts on needle 1, 30 sts on needle 2, and 15 sts on needle 3.
 Join rnd, being careful not twist sts.

Work k1, p1 rib for 1", then work in St st (k all rnds) for 1" more.

Cont in St st, work 2" in color B, then 2" in color A.

Change to color B and knit one rnd.

Next rnd: * K2tog, k3; rep from * around—needle 1: 12 sts; needle 2: 24 sts; needle 3: 12 sts.

K 6 more rnds.

Next rnd: K sts on needles 1 and 2.

| HEEL FLAP |

Note: Always slip st as if to purl and carry the yarn on the WS.

Working back and forth on needles 3 and 1, work as follows:

Next row (RS): * Sl 1, k1; rep from * across row, turn.

Next row: Sl 1, purl across row, turn.

Rep last 2 rows a total of 12 times.

Next row (RS): Sl 1, knit to end of row, turn.

| TURN HEEL |

Row 1 (WS): Sl 1, p13, p2tog, p1, turn.
Row 2: Sl 1, k5, k2tog, k1, turn.
Row 3: Sl 1, p6, p2tog, p1, turn.
Row 4: Sl 1, k7, k2tog, k1, turn.
Row 5: Sl 1, p8, p2tog, p1, turn.
Row 6: Sl 1, k9, k2tog, k1, turn.
Row 7: Sl 1, p10, p2tog, p1, turn.
Row 8: Sl 1, k11, k2tog, k1, turn.
Row 9: Sl 1, p12, p2tog, turn.
Row 10 (RS): Sl 1, k12, k2tog—7 sts rem on needle 3 and 7 sts rem on needle 1.

| FOOT |

With needle 1, pick up and k 12 sts along right side of heel—19 sts; with needle 2, k 24 sts for instep; with needle 3, pick up and k 12 sts along other side of heel, then k 7 sts from bottom of heel—19 sts. Mark the center of the heel for the beginning of the rnd.

Rnd 1: Knit.

Rnd 2: Needle 1: K to last 2 sts, k2tog; needle 2: Knit; needle 3: Ssk, k to end.

Rep rnds 1 and 2 until there are 12 sts on needle 1 and 12 sts on needle 3.

Cont to k all sts in rnd until foot measures 2" less than length of foot.

Slip sts onto a spare piece of yarn and try on the sock if desired.

| TOE |

Cut color B and change to color A.

Rnd 1: Knit.

Rnd 2: Needle 1: K to last 2 sts, k2tog; needle 2: Ssk, k to last 2 sts, k2tog; needle 3: Ssk, k to end.

Rep rnds 1 and 2 until 10 sts rem on needle 2, end having worked rnd 1.

K sts on needle 1. Slide sts from needle 3 onto needle 1—10 sts.

Cut yarn, leaving an 18" tail for grafting.

Graft toe using Kitchener stitch (see Abbreviations and Terms on page 146).

For Sock 2, reverse all colors.

---

chapter eight

the universal voice of craft
using crafts to express emotion

AS YOU BEGIN BRINGING YOUR KNITTING OUT INTO YOUR LOCAL COMMUNITY, YOU MAY SOON FIND THAT CRAFT HAS A REMARKABLE ABILITY TO HELP TRANSCEND CULTURAL DIFFERENCES. SOON after I started knitting in public, I discovered it could cross language barriers, making for a profound experience. One afternoon I was helping out with a charity yard sale, and when foot traffic got slow, I took out my knitting. A few moments after I began, a woman who had been sifting through the clothes hesitantly walked over to me, her eyes locked on the movement of my hands. When she got up close, she smiled and mimicked the motions of my hands knitting. She reached out and touched the scarf I was making and smiled again, then spoke to me in Spanish. Though we couldn't verbally communicate, we had a common understanding and connection through knitting.

Craft can be a profound way to transmit messages and emotions across the globe when we cannot communicate verbally or through written word—whether due to language barriers, lack of resources, or censorship. By choosing to craft specific items, such as political banners, memorial blankets, or pictorial tapestries, we are adding yet another layer to our crafting. Instead of just something to use for warmth or utility, craft can also take on a symbolic meaning. The triple use of intention, agenda, and end product creates a multitiered work that expresses our views, wants, and aesthetics all at once.

Handmade objects are able to resonate deeply with people because craft allows us to transform emotion into a tangible object. Just as music turns emotion into sound and writing turns emotion into the printed word, craft turns it into something we can hold in our hands and wrap around us, truly comforting our soul. I can hold the afghan you knitted row after row in the name of peace; I can hold your dissent in my hands. We can shout, we can cry, we can scream, but converting those energies into something real that we can grab onto is a unique way of turning feelings into something useful. It substitutes for all those words you can't quite form.

This chapter explores the emotion that can be expressed through our knitting and other needlecrafts: how it can be used to speak out when we can't, help us find support when we feel alone, and give us the strength to fight when we see injustice.

Rayna Fahey

RAYNA FAHEY LIVES IN AUSTRALIA AND BELIEVES IN THE POWER OF SEDITIOUS STITCHING. LEARN MORE AT RADICALCROSSSTITCH.COM

I'm one of those people who totally believes that everything you do is political. And I'd been an activist for about ten years before I started crafting. I started doing cross-stitch when I was pregnant, after I'd read all my books, couldn't stand watching TV anymore, and couldn't really move much either. I thought cross-stitch would be a nice, repetitive, boring thing for me to waste the months on. But after about a week, I couldn't help myself, and I started coming up with ways of politicizing my stitches. One thing led to another, and very soon I had a website and a pile of patterns made for radical cross-stitch.

A lot of my work has an overtly radical political message. I'm not really into being clever or witty. I just like cross-stitches that tell people how to run their lives! Most of what I create is of an anarcho-feminist nature, but there's also a strong indigenous sovereignty component in my stuff, because those are the things I'm most into. The stuff that doesn't have an overt political message is usually made out of reclaimed and upcycled materials, so I'm saving stuff from landfills. I think that's subversive too. We must beware the excessive consumerism of crafting!

As a women's studies graduate, I got to learn all about women's history and all these amazing people doing amazing stuff that we just don't hear about. Of course one of the things you never learn about is women's political art and craft. And there's so much of it out there, dating back centuries. So I try and draw on this herstory as much as I can. I'm stitching a series of feminist posters from different eras, because I think the artists of those times need to be honored as much as the activists.

The latest piece I designed and am currently stitching is an antique-inspired floral border surrounding the text "Don't bleed on the carpet." It's meant as an ironic tribute to all those revolting "Home sweet homes" out there. But it's also my little tribute to all the amazing women in the world who run households. It's such hard work and thanklessly unpaid. But it goes on no matter what, because it's such important work. We all need a place to call home. Somewhere where we can stop and be safe.

This piece is mostly dedicated to women living in the midst of war, who despite all obstacles still strive to provide a clean, tidy, safe space where their loved ones can rest before facing another day. The women who sew together scraps for their wee ones because they know how important it is for a two-year-old to have a cuddly friend. The women who dress in black and march for peace despite bullets and tear gas, all the while carrying giant handbags with keys and snacks and hankies for small runny noses.

Anger

Somewhere along the line, I forgot to get angry. Despite my beliefs in feminism, at some point in my life, I had begun to believe that showing my anger was impolite, unacceptable, and unfeminine. Although I can definitely be pushed to say angry words when heavily provoked, I always regret their harshness.

Something happens when we start to use our hands instead of our voices as a way to work through the anger. While words all too often come unprepared and unscripted, we must plan our knitting or needlework. By crafting our emotion, we create a conscious plan to express the feeling we are trying to get across and/or evoke. Instead of screaming, our work will hit viewers' eyes before their ears and allow a different sensory process of storytelling to emerge—with luck, one that can more peacefully facilitate change.

Chile's *arpilleristas* provide a profound example of how craft can express anger in powerful and moving ways. During the reign of Augusto Pinochet, the *arpilleristas* of Santiago made *arpilleras* (elaborate tapestries) to let people know about the injustices happening to their loved ones and their country. When their family members started disappearing, these women turned to their craft (because speaking out was too dangerous) to illustrate how they felt. In her book, *Scraps of Life*, Marjorie Agosin writes about the two reasons for the "evolution of the *arpilleristas*": "[T]he women have become more focused as to their direction and intentions and their horizons have widened because of their activity. Their intent is to use the arpillera as an alternative way of communicating since normal channels are blocked."

Using scraps of fabric and bits of thread, the mothers, sisters, and wives of *Los Desaparacidos* (The Disappeared) depicted stories and dreams about a situation entirely beyond their control. The only answers they could get about those who had disappeared without explanation was that no one knew where they were. As days became months and months became years, they heard nothing about the whereabouts of their loved ones. Unable to get closure and unsure whether the missing were still alive, being tortured, or killed and buried secretly, the *arpilleristas* created their colorful tapestries to help them continue on.

Textiles gave these women a voice; when they weren't allowed to speak, they could communicate their emotions through color, expressing their hopes and fears and anger stitch by stitch. As their *arpilleras* were sold illegally and shipped out of the country for sale on other continents, they informed people half a world away that in Chile, people were disappearing at an alarming rate. Craft became a way to cope with their extreme situation and reach out for help beyond their cultural and geographical boundaries.

Grief

How can we remember people we've lost if we don't have a photograph? In parts of Africa (and as part of African-American culture), memory jars are created to keep loved ones in the hearts and minds of those close to them. Small items belonging to the deceased are either placed in a jar or pot, or attached to it. The creation of the memory jar ensures that items of precious nostalgia are not lost, and that loved ones are not forgotten. There's something I really like about gathering tangible items from someone you loved who has passed on; they hold a different energy than a photograph and present a sort of three-dimensional memory. I've discussed how knitting can help us work through our emotions to help us process loss, heartbreak, and grief. This same principle can be applied on a larger scale. We can knit or sew to help others process their grief, whether individually or in a larger group.

In times of emotional upheaval, handmade objects can provide a wealth of comfort, especially because we sometimes shy away from grief, internalizing our own, ignoring others', generally pushing it away. By honoring and staying with our feelings of sadness, we have the opportunity to heal and move forward.

Many people find that making bereavement quilts made from the clothes of their deceased loved one helps them to process the loss and cherish the memories. According to artist Sherri Wood, this process gives the quilter "a container to enter in grief for a period of time." It becomes a tangible, visual way to work through sadness and a flood of emotions during a difficult time, putting more meaning into the end product. The maker can (hopefully) come out of the experience with a deeper understanding and appreciation of someone who is no longer around but is still held dear.

The idea of taking old clothes and breathing new life into them is another way of taking time out to honor someone and their life. Unlike a prized ice chest or heirloom sideboard, clothes retain the smell, feel, and shape of their owners. A patch where a small hole was covered, a tear mended by hands years ago, worn-out knees. More than idle castoffs, clothes reflect a person's taste and character, and hold much more of his or her essence than most other possessions. When pondering how to best remember someone, having a look at his or her wardrobe might be a good first start. You might want to consider using the garments to create something like a pillow or a blanket.

You may find that crafting with other types of belongings is more appropriate to your own situation. Maybe your loved one liked model airplanes and you can make them into a mobile. Maybe beads from a bracelet can be turned into another bracelet or a necklace. Maybe there is something special you can take from their possessions to transform into something new to keep the memory of someone you've lost always close at hand.

Otto von Busch

Otto von Busch splits his time between Sweden and Turkey. You can find his work at selfpassage.org.

Central to my practice is how to engage with fashion, to "hack" it in some way. Fashion is both a liberating and an oppressive system. It can help us to dress apart and to celebrate the possibility for change, both personal and social. But it is also a nonparticipative and "interpassive" system, dictating the decrees of the constant new. It thrives on being unattainable, constantly somewhere else, just beyond reach, something that creates anxiety and a sense of constant lack. Nevertheless, it is this paradox that is the dynamic energy of the fashion logic that powers the system. This makes it fascinating to work with. Not to overthrow, resist, or defy fashion, but instead to try to tune it, bend it, hack it—to liberate some of the positive energies within. An engaged activism of craft, a fashion-affirming craftivism.

Central to this "hacking" is the development of craftsmanship and sharpening the tools for action. We can use fashion as a workshop for collective enablement, where community members share their methods and experiences to become not only good crafters but also good fashionistas. We can use it as a way of understanding the hands-on skills required to make things, as well as the image making, styling, and logic that make fashion run so powerfully in our society; we can plug into this vivid energy with the aim of social change. We can also use fashion to create small scenes, base communities of fashion and craft, and from there open our practices into larger communities. Where we take action can range from the kitchen table up to the factories within the fashion industry itself. This way we might liberate parts of fashion from a phenomenon of cultural dictations and anxiety to instead become a collective experience of empowerment through engaged craft. The sewing machine can become an instrument for liberation, and the development of fashion-related craftsmanship a path to freedom.

Joy

Along with emotions that can weigh us down, we also need to express our more festive moods. Knitting can be done in the name of a new baby, a wedding, a birthday, or any other occasion that might be worth remembering. While craft can help us process sadness and confusion, it can also be a celebration of the goodness that life can hold. Use your knitting to help bring joy into a stranger's life at times of great happiness. Children's charities collect handmade items such as clothing, blankets, and toys for wee ones around the world. Unfortunately there is always a great number of children in need, so the need for donations is universal. Perhaps you have a bit of yarn that can be transformed into a knitted toy, a scrap of fabric that can make a nice doll, or some random old sweaters to be felted and given a new life as a cozy blanket.

Many hospitals have programs that collect caps for newborns. While some babies are instantly showered with presents from that first breath, many others do not have that luxury. The presentation of a soft hat, made by hand with the celebration of life in mind, is a wonderful way to be welcomed into the community and the world. Hats for infants take almost no time to make and can be whipped up in an hour or so with less than a skein of yarn. If this idea appeals to you, check with local hospitals to see if they collect caps for newborns; if they don't, you might even get them to start. The only limit to a project such as this is that the hat should be machine-washable and made from yarn that will not be itchy.

Sometimes it's hard to even think about how to express what you're feeling, but you can project your emotions outward with your hands. Start a piece with a spark of an idea and then work out the rest in the production. You can follow the emotion that you're feeling and work without knowing what the outcome will be. While this has enormous therapeutic and meditative benefits, it can also moor you to your beliefs. Craft can be reflexive, a mirror between inside and outside, going in both directions. What you make shows the world what you're feeling, and what you take from the world, you internalize in your craft. In this respect, creativity can really become a channel of positivity and spirit as you work without premeditation.

Knitting for Good Actions

| Expressing Your Emotion through Knitting |

What would a tapestry of your life look like? Consider the stories and scenes you'd illustrate, the colors you would use, the materials that would best express your personality. Would you divulge secrets or stay safe? Would you want to show it just to your family or to the public?

| Using Every Scrap |

Not only does using up your yarn stash eliminate waste and clutter in your home, but it can also be turned into something that brings joy to others. Go through your supply and collect leftover bits from skeins and abandoned projects. What could you make with them? A stripey tiny blanket for a preemie? Leg warmers for a greyhound? A squishy toy for a baby to cuddle? Try thinking about your stash as a source of opportunity instead of just loose odds and ends.

Manos Asymmetric Vest

Designed by Judith Shangold

Clothing that can provide substantial warmth is always needed by various charities around the world. Making and donating this vest can help keep someone layered up and warm against chilly winter winds.

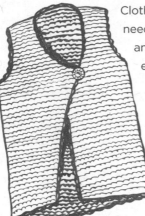

| SIZES |

Petite (Small, Medium, Large)

| FINISHED MEASUREMENTS |

Finished chest: 33 (37, 41, 45)"
Finished length: 20 1/2 (22 1/2, 24, 26)"

| YARN |

Manos del Uruguay Wool Clàsica (100% wool; 138 yards/100 grams): 4 (4, 5, 5) skeins #53 Mulberry (MC); 1 skein #55 Olive (CC)

| NEEDLES |

One pair straight needles size US 9 (5.5 mm)
   Change needle size if necessary to obtain correct gauge.

| NOTIONS |

Crochet hook size F, one button 1 1/2" in diameter (button shown from zecca.net)

| GAUGE |

16 sts and 24 rows = 4" (10 cm) in pattern stitch

| BASKET-WEAVE STITCH |

Row 1 and all WS rows: Purl.
   Rows 2 and 4: K2, *p2, k2; rep from *.
   Rows 6 and 8: P2, *k2, p2; rep from *.
   Repeat rows 1–8 for pat.

| BACK |

With MC, CO 66 (74, 82, 90) sts. Work rows 1–8 of basket-weave st 9 (10, 11, 12) times, end having worked row 1 of pat—piece measures approximately 12 (13 1/2, 15, 16 1/2)". Shape armholes: Keeping to pat, bind off 6 sts beg of next 2 rows. Dec 1 st each edge every RS row 4 times as follows: K1, ssk, work in pat to last 3 sts, k2tog, k1—46 (54, 62, 70) sts remain. Work even in pat until armhole measures 8 (8 1/2, 8 1/2, 9)", end WS row. Shape shoulders: Bind off knitwise 10 (13, 17, 20) sts beg of next 2 rows. Bind off rem sts.

| LEFT FRONT |

With MC, CO 34 (38, 42, 46) sts. Work in pat until piece measures same as back to armhole, end row 1 of pat. Shape armhole and neck, next row (RS): Keeping to pat, bind off 6 sts, work rem sts. Dec 1 st each edge every RS row 4 times as follows: K1, ssk work to last 3 sts, k2tog, k1. Cont to dec at neck edge *only* every RS row 3 more times, then every 4th row 7 (8, 8, 9) times—10 (13, 17, 20) sts remain. Work even in pat until piece measures same as back to shoulder, end WS row. Bind off knitwise.

| RIGHT FRONT |

With MC, CO 26 (28, 30, 32) sts. Work in pat, CO 1 st beg of every 4th row 18 (20, 22, 24) times, adding new sts into pat, end row 8 of pat—44 (48, 52, 56) sts.

Shape armhole and neck, next row (WS): Keeping to pat, bind off 6 sts, work rem sts. Next row: Bind off 10 sts, work to last 3 sts, k2tog, k1. Dec 1 st each edge every RS row 3 times as follows: K1, ssk, work to last 3 sts, k2tog, k1. Cont to dec at neck edge *only* every RS row 4 more times, then every 4th row 7 (8, 8, 9) times—10 (13, 17, 20) sts remain. Work even in pat until piece measures same as back to shoulder, end WS row. Bind off knitwise.

| FINISHING |

Sew shoulder and side seams.

Edging: With crochet hook and CC, right side facing, start at right shoulder seam and work a row of single crochet across back of neck and around front and bottom edges, working 3 sc into corner spaces; sl st into first sc.

Rnd 1: *Ch4, skip 3 sc, sc into next st; rep from * around, sl st into first st.

Note: If last repeat is not 4 sts, work fewer ch and skip fewer sc.

Rnd 2: Ch1, * work (sc, ch2, dc, sc) into ch 4 space; rep from * around, sl st to first st, cut yarn and pull end through loop.

Armhole edging: With crochet hook and CC, right side facing, start at side seam and work a row of sc around armhole, sl st to first sc. Work rnd 1 of edging as above.

Cut yarn, pull end through loop.

Sew on button, aligning it with one of the crochet edge eyelets for buttonhole.

Handwash garment in warm water with small amount of dishwashing liquid. Rinse. Wrap in towel to remove water or run through the spin cycle in washing machine. Lay flat to dry.

chapter nine

drop stitches, not bombs
activism and knitting

ONE OF THE THINGS THAT I HAVE BEEN DEEPLY INVOLVED IN OVER THE PAST FEW YEARS IS THE PROMOTION OF *CRAFTIVISM*, WHICH IS THE POINT WHERE *CRAFTS* AND *ACTIVISM* MEET. BY TAKING TWO SEEMINGLY DISPArate words that are negatively stereotyped in their own ways (craft can be seen as dull or old-fashioned, activism as violent or radical) and combining them to create a new word, *craftivism* strikes out into new territory. In 2003, I started using the term after a friend came up with it during a knitting circle. I soon discovered that others had also come up with the concept, pointing to a shared frustration about issues like consumerism, materialism, anti–green living, a lack of personal expression, and overconsumption. It was a topic that had piqued interest. The fact that several different people in geographically separate parts of the world had similar ideas around the same time spoke to the fact that this convergence, if properly harnessed, could be more powerful than we ever thought possible.

Theorist Nicole Burisch sees craftivism as "emerging out of the renewed interest in social justice/activist issues that came in response to global trade issues/ antiglobalization politics of the early 2000s (and increased media attention for the WTO protests in Seattle, and take-back-the streets parties, etc., at that time). Alongside those, it seems there was a lot of interest in using alternative strategies for protest and action: often those that employ a degree of humor, accessibility, and play (costuming, street theater, raging grannies, radical cheerleaders, etc.)."

Sage Adderley

SAGE ADDERLEY IS A TATTOO ARTIST, CRAFTER, AND MOTHER WHO RESIDES IN GEORGIA. SHE ALSO RUNS SWEET CANDY

DISTRO (EYECANDYZINE.COM), WHICH SELLS ZINES AND HAND-MADE CRAFTS.

Creating with my hands has always been one of the most natural ways to express my thoughts and emotions. When I craft, I am releasing the energy within myself that needs to be channeled outward. Craft has been a powerful tool in my life and has carried me through phases when I was dealing with major issues such as domestic violence, single parenting, and poor body image. Not only did I motivate myself, but I motivated others as well.

In the past few years, I have found a community of fellow crafters who have similar feelings about the power of craft. We have gathered together; each of us busy with our chosen craft. You can feel the power we radiate together while our minds and hands stay focused. To craft is to empower ourselves to be heard. Our opinions are vital, and with our craft, we can impact our community in a positive manner.

My children craft when they want to tell a loved one something special or when they feel the world needs to hear their small but important voices. Through craft, we can support each other in personal and political gatherings. We craft for ourselves, for charities, and for a better tomorrow.

Starting Out

What can you, just one person, do for the world? Faced with such an enormous question, you may very well answer, "Not much." But I think we owe it to the world and to ourselves to use our creativity and passion to foster and build kindness.

There are always changes we can make in our daily lives that positively affect others, whether directly or indirectly. Karina Tipton and Jenn Sturiale believe it's the small things that help us create lasting change. Their website, Tinychoices.com, is based on the small choices we can make to help the planet. Their message: "Choose to consume less. Choose to make your own things, if you can. Choose to save your money for a season by wearing your older clothes a little longer in order to save up for something of higher quality that may last longer and that is made from materials you feel confident about environmentally." Once we get in the habit of making tiny ethical choices, perhaps we'll be able to graduate to larger and more influential actions.

Beyond providing people with basic needs such as food, water, clothing, and shelter, creativity is the most important thing we can pass on to those in need. Being able to embrace your own creativity is just a step away from hope. We've seen how we can use our creative energy to improve others' lives by teaching a skill, forming relationships, and making donations. Isn't that good enough? Of course! Just by creating one item and donating it to charity you are helping someone, which is working toward the greater good.

When we make the leap to connect our immediate community to the global community, it can seem a bit daunting. But the global community comes from the same place as any smaller community, it's just not as geographically limited. The key to working toward the greater good is knowing what to give and when to give it. Some of us burn out after an hour or two of tutoring or mentoring; others volunteer in poverty-stricken locations for hours, devoting round-the-clock care to the sick and hungry. Once we know what we can give, our power lies in that sphere. If we're lucky, that sphere will become larger, expanding our capacity to want and need to work toward making the world a better place.

What resources and talents can you share to make a few people's lives a little better? Although writing a check is a good thing, what if you either don't believe in throwing money at a problem or don't really have much money to throw around? Consider the basic needs that we all have—food, water, and shelter. Create items that address these needs. In realizing how grateful you are to have a warm sweater to wrap around yourself, you understand how fully delicious it feels, and you can start thinking about sharing that warmth with others. When you bring it all back to a level of humanity, suddenly the vastness begins to fall away.

Knit to express the need for change by knitting a protest banner to hang, share, or wear; have a knit-in at a protest; share your cultural/political feelings in a piece you create; or talk to other people in your community about using their creative gifts toward the greater good. When you can, knit to create change by making items for charities that help support your cause, starting your own charitable organization, or using a skill set you have to benefit others. Just go where your heart and hands take you and hold on.

You can use a cultural stereotype (that craft isn't dangerous) to help further a message of your choice. Use it to wake people up, to lead them into action. By shifting the paradigm, you get them to think, which is a large part of moving toward change. Change is something that we have to allow internally before we can express it externally. If we feel passionate about a cause, and especially if we understand and have processed that passion, we will be able to do more than just yell slogans; we will be able to incorporate it into our lives and work in other ways to get conversations about the problem and solutions flowing. The joy of finding causes you really believe in is discovering how others feel about the same things. Once you've expanded your own mind, you can then listen to others and build and grow and change and evolve. You've just got to want it.

So what if you want it? What do you do? What if you have the energy, but don't have the ideas? Start reading the news and paying attention, see where there are needs in this world, and what needs you can best help to meet. It doesn't matter if you can only fill a tiny bit of a giant hole; you are contributing something, which moves everyone one step closer to the ultimate goal.

WENDY TREMAYNE WRITES THE "RE:FITTED" COLUMN IN *CRAFT* MAGAZINE, WHICH FEATURES INNOVATIVE DIY REUSE PROJECTS. SHE IS ALSO THE FOUNDER OF SWAP-O-RAMA-RAMA—A WORLDWIDE, NONPROFIT CLOTHING SWAP AND SERIES OF DIY EVENTS DESIGNED TO DEPOPULARIZE CONSUMERISM.

In 2000, I left my last "job" and began to live on my own terms and work only for myself doing projects that were meaningful to me. I was specifically interested in where meaning is derived in a society that is 100 percent commodified. Since it's through consumerism that we as individuals experience this commodification, I began to deeply examine consumerism, and I made a commitment to "deconstruct the consumer." This ultimately led me to create Swap-O-Rama-Rama and brought me to my conclusions about meaning and value and my credo that in today's time the "maker" (the person who makes his or her world rather than buys it) is the modern revolutionary.

To understand consumerism and value, I decided to live for one year on barter, no money. For each area of my life, I had to be very creative about how I would get what I needed without using money. As a musician, I played gigs at venues that served food; I worked out arrangements with roommates that I would provide things other than rent money. I wound up making them a lot of stuff like blankets, creating a garden, and so on. For my wardrobe, I chose to create a clothing swap. After organizing a few swaps in my apartment, it seemed clear that there was an impulse to be more creative. And those swaps became the mechanism that I would use for my task of deconstructing the consumer.

Contemplation led me to some key components:

The store environment reduces intimacy. People either go shopping alone and stay alone, or they go with a friend and talk only to that person. At Swap-O-Rama-Rama, there are no mirrors; this is to remedy the distance the shopping mall has created. When people realize there are no mirrors, they turn to a stranger and ask, "How do I look?" Then another stranger from across the room will say, "This is so you!" and hold up a garment.

Branding is divisive. Current branding on clothing creates distinct social groups that divide people by the size of their wallet, not the breadth of their creativity. At Swap-O-Rama-Rama, we provide new labels that say "100% modified by me" to cover existing branding and mark the newly transformed garments with a celebration of their new owners' creativity.

Shopping is not creative. Only a few rare people in our society are creators: engineers, clothing designers, scientists, and so forth. This is counterintuitive and ultimately reduces human beings to cogs. Every human being was born a creator. Swap-O-Rama-Rama invites people to become creators again.

Consumer goods lead to trash. A hundred years ago, we made—or someone we knew made—everything we owned and there was no trash! Objects were imbued with meaning. At Swap-O-Rama-Rama, we transform the stale manufactured goods made by machines into things that have meaning by changing them and adding human intention.

Making builds knowledge. Makers do not make good consumers. Commodified culture breeds ignorance. All makers quickly learn that they must explore materials and become educated about them: their origins, how they're made, where they're made.

Steps toward Change

Here are some ideas about what you can do to change the world.

Explore

Travel across the country or across the globe. By seeing yourself as a true entity of the world, you can start to identify the ways you can help. Maybe you can go home and tell people about the new things you saw, or return to a country that spoke to you to do volunteer work, or make something for needy people you find in your travels. The first step in helping the world become a better place is to see yourself in the world and to decide what you can contribute.

Learn about Other Cultures and Crafts

One of the things that surprised me most about knitting was to learn that there were different ways of approaching the craft in different parts of the world. While this may seem naive, I was startled to find that people purled differently in Iceland and that some patterns were part of a country's cultural tradition. Suddenly each sweater from Ireland or yard of fabric from South America opened up a wealth of information about the needs of different cultures and how the utility of craft allows for subtle changes to be made out of necessity and availability. Something about looking at handmade cloth around the world solidified the inherent likenesses we all share instead of the differences. Which, when you think of it, is pretty magical.

Express Your Intentions and Beliefs

Use your craft to express your beliefs. Through tangible, handmade objects, we can better connect with those around us, who might not know how to strike up a conversation at random but can certainly talk about what you're making or have made. One of the gifts of the handmade is that by practicing it (or wearing it) in public, you provide an opportunity for conversation with people of similar interests. Taking the time to knit a protest sign—rather than make a poster—reinforces your voice and actually shows that not only do you mean what you say, you *mean* it. It takes your feelings and turns them into something other than a piece of cardboard. It will last longer and speak louder.

Some of the most successful protest pieces I have seen at rallies have been made by hand. It's easier to talk to someone who is wearing a hand-knitted, antiwar sweater or standing in the middle of a cardboard tank than it is to one of the thousands of people holding preprinted signs that protesters like to hand out. If you're lucky, you might even get the chance to talk with some people who don't feel the same way as you about the issue. Not that you're going to necessarily change their minds, but conversation is a way forward, especially when it comes to "hot button" issues.

Live Fiercely and Bravely

Thanks to a mix tape from a friend, I discovered the music of Nusrat Fateh Ali Khan. At first, I just liked the fact that since I had no idea what he was saying in Urdu, I wouldn't get distracted. But as I began to listen to twenty-minute songs that all built up in the same fashion, but with different beats and words,

I was curious about what compelled this music that seemed like bottled energy. After listening for a while, something in me just wanted to spin and spin and spin, like a whirling dervish, and to create energy. After a little research, I learned that Khan was a singer in the qawwali tradition, a Pakistani form of worship. Each song was composed of different parts and built up as the sense of prayer and devotion heightened.

They weren't singing for financial gain or fame or anything besides joy and devotion. Why they were doing it was an integral part of the whole experience; it was more than entertainment or practice. And there was a sense of bravery and fierceness behind it that was more admirable than nearly any music I had ever heard. It was loud to express faith, not loud just to be heard. Without fail, somewhere around the fifteen-minute mark of the longer songs, I would always be overcome with an almost overwhelming sense of joy and peace and the magic that comes from getting lost in creativity. Despite speaking a different language and practicing a different religion, the singers' message came through boldly and was a clear reminder to live and create bravely.

Let the creative process take you. You may begin with one idea and end up with something totally different, or be left with a total mess, but by following the generation of a new thought, you are daring to trust and be bold, if only for a few moments.

What can we do for the world? We can be in it. We can trust our creativity and our passion enough to honor it and share it. In exploring cultures and expanding your knowledge, you are working toward the perpetuation of craft; by not being afraid to mix your influences, you are letting craft breathe of and on its own.

Projects for a Better Planet

There are currently individuals doing works of radical craft all over the world—entirely too many to write about here. But to give you an idea of what people are doing with their political craft—how they're using it to voice their opinions, gain employment, and stand up—here are just a few examples of some artists and crafters I greatly admire.

Otto von Busch

By providing tutorials on how to re-create our wardrobes, and therefore "hack" into the production of clothing, von Busch has managed to help us try to change the ways we look at clothes and textile production. While his work is highly theoretical, it stems outward to things we can all fight against. By encasing his tutorials in a theoretical framework, von Busch is holistically challenging the system, both the producers themselves (by restructuring their clothes) and the makers (by forcing them to think about why reconstructing a wardrobe is a liberation of both mind and body). We are all masters of our wardrobe, in a sense, our own factories as we tackle our clothes. In an interview with online zine *We Make Money Not Art,* von Busch states, comparing the wardrobe hackers with heretics, "The heretic is not an atheist, but someone hacking the institutional and hierarchical interpretation of the faith. Like the hacker, modder, or tinkerer the heretic is keeping the power on, not renouncing or opposing the core or energy of a system. Using faith for liberation and empowerment. This approach can also be taken in fashion. Not boycotting fashion or scorning it as 'the emperor's new clothes,' but instead celebrating the magic and desire flowing through that system, reconnecting it to empower instead of regarding it as an enslaving culture." Von Busch wants us to use the energy drifting through modes of mass production for our own experiments in creativity.

By wrapping up what we can do to fashion in modern culture, von Busch stresses the importance of making our wardrobes our own. Instead of concentrating on what the factories give us and their negative sides, he highlights the joy that can come from alternative modes of production and shows us how we can retool these in our own lives. We can use von Busch's work as inspiration to discover what goes into the production of our clothes. Is it a system we agree with? Are there elements of production that cause us frustration or sadness or glee? What can we take from opening up and looking into the inner workings of factories and big retailers? Does it seem like the work of people or more like cogs moving on a machine? What could make the process less alienating?

Stitch for Senate

Artist and theorist Cat Mazza created her website, microRevolt.org, to "investigate the dawn of sweatshops in early industrial capitalism" and to inform others about "the current crisis of global expansion and the feminization of labor." Her most recent project is Stitch for Senate, which speaks out against the conflicts in Iraq and Afghanistan by combining theory with visual art. By joining intricate thoughts with handmade items, Mazza's work helps viewers make connections between their personal experiences and those of individuals who are experiencing injustice, thus elucidating how alike we all are. The Stitch for Senate project mixes history with present-day scenarios, linking two similar situations. During the world wars of the last century, women knitted as a way to support the soldiers who were fighting in colder climates. They produced socks, hats, sweaters, and helmet liners. For the current conflicts in Iraq and Afghanistan, Mazza is collecting helmet liners based on a WWII pattern, one for each senator. (In the interest of full disclosure, I have already knitted mine.) What struck me most about this particular project was the bridge between past and present. Each liner will be sent to a state senator, who will then be asked to either keep the liner or donate it to a soldier overseas.

By creating garments for individual soldiers, she's putting a face on the war. By creating on a personal level, these pieces serve to remind us that instead of something that's just happening on our television (and computer) screens, the war affects the lives of real, breathing people—not pawns in a game, but human beings just like you and me.

The strength of this project lies in the personal connection it forces us to make. What I say may go in one ear and out the other, or be drowned out by those around me (whether they're agreeing or disagreeing), but acts of craft resonate deeper than words. Craft takes more processing as our minds translate what we're seeing. We can ignore what we hear more easily than we can ignore a visual piece of art.

Mazza attacks the problems of the current American conflict by bringing it down to a level that is easily understandable—using history's past experiences of knitting for war and creating items that soldiers need. By producing utile objects that have political purpose, her project garners more attention. And by using an item as simple as a helmet liner to symbolize the problems with conflicts in Iraq and Afghanistan, she's bringing us just a little bit closer to a world that seems far away and removed from our everyday lives.

Penguin Jumpers Project

Although this project is no longer taking donations, it's a great reminder that not just people need help when disasters take place. When the call was made online for donations of knitted sweaters to keep in oil-spill response kits on tiny Bruny Island in Tasmania, the response was huge. Especially when people realized that these weren't just any knitted sweaters, but tiny versions for the island inhabitants that can be harmed in the event of an oil spill—penguins. This project managed to do several different things: it foresaw a need, filled it, and raised awareness for the dangers animals face because of oil spills.

The project was so successful because it asked for a creative solution to a potential problem. The unusual nature of the request (small sweaters for penguins) led to rapidly increased interest. This increased awareness extended to what can happen to any wildlife during an oil spill and highlighted the fragility of our environment. Instead of just showing photographs of injured animals, it offered an example of how humans can help directly.

Condom Amulets

Naomi Dagen Bloom wants to talk about sex. After learning about the rising number of women over fifty who were contracting AIDS, Dagen Bloom decided to raise awareness about a problem that many people never even knew existed. While there is much media attention given to the need for younger people to have safe sex and how continents like Africa need more HIV education, there was little about how women of "a certain age" need to be safe too.

In her zine, *Knit a Condom Amulet*, she reminds us that, "according to the Center for Disease Control and Prevention (CDC), the number of Americans over 50 who are infected with HIV has grown over 5 times (16,300 people in 1995, to 90,600 in 2003). While seniors represent about 14% of people with HIV, senior women represent 18%." She provides individuals with a pattern for knitting a condom amulet (a pouch to be worn around the neck that holds a condom).

The amulets are a wake-up call. While I have an idea of how rapidly the rate of HIV is growing in Africa, I was floored to learn about the growing rate of the same disease in older American women. Dagen Bloom makes people aware of this issue and also fights against the common perception that once you get old, sex stops. She is helping women keep safe and ensuring that the word is spread, instead of HIV.

While I have tried to capture a few examples of the political craft that spans the globe, it can never be close to the scope of what's out there. Right now people are creating works of political art that they can't show out of fear of being hurt, ashamed, or worse. We may think that problems like the people disappearing in Chile (see chapter 8) are in the past, but similar activities are happening somewhere, and people are creating in order to fight the injustice in their own quiet way. It may take time for us to see their works so we can begin to understand more about their experiences, just as the tapestries of the *arpilleristas* had to be smuggled out of Chile before the rest of the world knew what was happening. Although I know there is some amazing political work out there, I also know there are loads of pieces I won't see—and may never see—given the political climates of some places in the world.

That's the hard part. Knowing that somewhere someone is making things that are born of frustration and anger, but due to geography, they are unable to express these feelings publicly. I gain strength knowing that somewhere someone is knitting or weaving or sewing or tying or gluing or beading in secret, and it is my hope that one day they will be free. It is for them that I make my feelings known via the handmade, because these struggles are hard-won and arduous, and just because we can ignore them, doesn't mean they'll disappear.

Knowing that there are organizations and groups helping people find ways to make a living out of something of their own creation makes me that much more determined to work on creating a handmade microeconomy where I live. I hope that although it may not be fully sustainable, it will help spread the word that there are other ways of living than just the easy route.

Asking questions, needing to know answers, looking for truth, wanting others to have their basic needs met as we do—all these things facilitate political craft. I've mentioned a few groups here that do great work, but it's just a small sampling of what's going on. Broken down into tiny pieces, the world is full of people, not just separate entities many time zones apart. And as people, we have the chance to work toward a better world, and that thought is kept manageable and doable once we see that although the problems of the world are vast, there are small ways we can reach out and start to help people. I may only knit ten scarves in one year that go to charity, but that means that somewhere ten more people are warmer. When it's all added up, we can make a difference.

Knitting for Good Actions

| Finding the Activist Within |

Most of us are activists, even though we may not label ourselves as such. But why must *activist* be such a dirty word? Think about past issues that have caused you to speak out, act out, or be otherwise compelled to make a change. They can be as tiny as getting your family to turn off the water while they brush their teeth or writing a letter to the editor to voice your opinion. It's not about the size of the action, it's about what caused you to take action in the first place.

Is there anything at work or at home that you'd like to change for ethical, political, or consumerist reasons? Maybe incorporate paper recycling into your current recycling regimen? Or get your company to use more sustainable cups instead of Styrofoam?

| It's All in the Details |

Now that you've come up with a few ideas for things you could change to make your environment, house, community, or place of employment a little better, pick the one that most appeals to you. Commit to actually doing it for a week. When the week is over, see if that one tiny change made a difference in how you think about other possible tiny changes. Hopefully, it will! If it doesn't, you've changed your habits for the better for a short time, and all those good actions add up.

Mossy Jacket

Designed by fawn pea (f.pea designs)

Whenever I see a pattern for a baby something or other that says it's a very special something or other, that usually means it is hyperruffled, tied with a hundred ribbons, or made from artisan-spun cashmere. I think this little jacket is a very special baby gift because it's just really nice. It has a funky, off-center button band; it's cute, colorful, fairly quick to knit, and made from merino wool—a little bit chichi, but not ridiculously so.

The jacket is knit top-down, all in one piece, and the yarn is knit tightly on needles slightly smaller than called for to make a nice winter jacket for an infant. Using just two buttons makes it easy to get on and off. (Note: I am a really loose knitter, so the needle size might not work for you. Make sure you do a swatch to get the correct gauge for this project.)

| SIZES |

6 mos (12 mos, 18 mos)

| FINISHED MEASUREMENTS |

Finished chest: 21 (23, 24 1/2)"
Finished length: 10 (11 1/2, 13)"

| YARN |

Classic Elite Beatrice (100% merino wool; 63 yards/50 grams): 3 skeins #3215 Aspen Grove (MC); 1 skein #3285 Autumn Hillside (CC)

| NEEDLES |

One 26" circular needle size US 9
(5.5 mm)

One 26" circular needle size US
10 (6 mm)

One set double pointed needles
(dpns) size US 9 (5.5 mm)

One set double pointed needles
(dpns) size US 10 (6 mm)

Change needle size if necessary
to obtain correct gauge.

| NOTIONS |

Scrap yarn as st holders for
sleeves, two buttons 1" in diameter, stitch markers, tapestry
needle, pin as marker

| GAUGE |

14 sts and 20 rows = 4" (10 cm)
in Stockinette stitch (St st) with
larger needles

| NOTES |

Garment is worked in one piece
starting at the neck.

Make all increases (inc) by knitting
into the front and back of the stitch.

| SEED STITCH |

Row 1: *K1, p1; rep from *.
Row 2: *P1, k1; rep from *.
Rep rows 1 and 2.

| JACKET |

Starting at neck and using larger
needles and MC, CO 3 sts for Right
Front, place marker (M); CO 8 (8,
9) sts for Right Sleeve, place M;
CO 14 (15, 16) sts for Back, place
M; CO 8 (8, 9) sts for Left Sleeve,
place M; CO 1 st for Left Front—34
(35, 38) sts.

Row 1 (RS): Inc in first st, slip
M, inc, *k to 1 st before next M,
inc, sl M, inc, rep from * to last
st, inc in last st—9 sts increased.

Row 2: Purl.

Row 3: *K to 1 st before M, inc, sl
M, inc, rep from * to last st, inc in
last st—9 sts increased.

Row 4: Purl.

Rep rows 3 and 4 once more—61
(62, 65) sts.

Next row (RS): Place pin at
beginning of row and work row
3 again, CO 4 (5, 6) sts at end of
row—74 (76, 80) sts.

Next row: Purl.

Next row: K, inc 1 st before
and after each M—8 sts increased.

Rep last 2 rows 5 (6, 7) more
times—122 (132, 144) sts.

Mossy Jacket (Continued)

| DIVIDE FOR SLEEVES |

Next RS row: K 11 (12, 13) sts for Left Front, remove M; place 28 (30, 33) sleeve sts on a length of scrap yarn; CO 1 st, remove M, inc in next st, knit rem 33 (36, 39) sts for back, remove M, place 28 (30, 33) sleeve sts on scrap yarn, CO 1 st, remove next M, inc in next st, k rem 20 (22, 24) sts for Right Front—70 (76, 82) sts for body.

| BODY |

Cont to work in St st, until piece measures 9 (10 1/2, 12)" from CO edge, end WS row. Cut MC.

Next row (RS): Change to smaller needles and CC and k 1 row.

K 4 rows in Seed st. Bind off loosely in pat.

| SLEEVES |

Slip sts on holder to dpns, distributing them evenly on 4 needles. Join MC, pick up and k 1 st at the underarm, k rem sts—29 (31, 34) sts. Place marker and join, being careful not to twist sts. K 3 more rnds.

Next rnd, dec rnd: K to last 2 sts, k2tog. K 3 rnds.

Rep dec rnd on every 4th rnd 5 more times—23 (25, 28) sts rem.

Work even until sleeve measures 6 (6 1/2, 7)" or desired length from underarm. Cut MC.

Change to smaller needles and CC. K 1 rnd.

Work 4 rnds in Seed st. Bind off loosely in pat.

Repeat for second sleeve.

| FINISHING |

Button Bands: With smaller circular needles and CC, RS facing, start at pin and pick up and k 30 (34, 39) sts along left front edge. Work 4 rows in Seed st. Bind off in pat. With RS facing, pick up and k 30 (34, 39) sts along right front edge. Work 2 rows in Seed st. Next row, work buttonholes: Keeping to pat, work 2 sts, yo, work 2 tog, work 5 sts, yo, work 2 tog, work rem sts. Work 1 more row. Bind off in pat.

Collar: With smaller needles and CC, RS facing, pick up and k 4 sts from buttonhole band, 10 (12, 12) sts across right front neck edge, 8 (8, 9) sts across top of right sleeve, 14 (15, 16) sts across back neck, 8 (8, 9) sts across top of left sleeve, 6 (7, 8) sts along left front neck and 4 sts along top of button band—54 (58, 62) sts. Work 3 rows in Seed st. Bind off in pat.

Sew on buttons. Weave in loose ends.

afterword

DURING AN E-MAIL DIALOGUE ABOUT CRAFT AND ITS STRENGTHS, ENVIRONMENTAL ARTIST BRYANT HOLSENBECK WROTE, "THINK ABOUT IT—A HUNDRED YEARS AGO, MANY MORE PEOPLE HAD TO weave their clothes, kill their sheep, chop their wood. There was no need for gyms, people were getting plenty of exercise just living their lives. For me, making, understanding how things are made or grow for that matter, has been a life's passion. I like to pick up a leaf and see how the veins grow from the stem or how a young flower unfurls from its bud. My own work has grown from being a craftsperson—potter turned basket maker to someone who does work that chronicles the waste stream. My utilitarian craft has become art. I think every act of making is an act of revolution. It is stopping the rush of time—time here, time there—hurry up, hurry up. And taking time to understand how something is made and making it with meditation." Even though I met Bryant as I was finishing this book, her approach to creativity was a testament to the power of craft. And I believe that if you can end a project as strongly as you started it, you're on the right path.

Each action we take has the possibility to gain momentum, both in our own actions and in those of others. By truly *being* the change we want to see in this world, even if it seems like the smallest of changes, we are putting energy toward that momentum, helping it gain speed. By starting out with small things, such as what one person can do, it's then easier to build up to big things, like what a whole planet can do.

If you truly participate in acts of change or goodness or charity, then it's not about rallying the troops and getting everyone to see things your way. The truest aspect of a good deed does not need reciprocity to complete the process. Give *if* you want to give, *how* you can give, *as much* as you want to give. The idea of this book is to get you thinking about small changes you can make or tiny ideas you can use to make your life and the lives of others a bit better. The goal is to explore different ways to view and express your creativity. When asked about how craft affects her life, author and designer Tsia Carson writes, "on a personal level two reasons fuel my making. One is the promise of the alchemical transformation of turning base materials into gold. I can take something like yarn and turn it into something, anything almost—a lampshade, a scarf, an opening up of imagination. The other is that the act of making as a spiritual practice. It is divine in its essence. It is the process that carries the intentionality. In the intention is the power." By expanding your own views of what it means to craft and be creative, you have more room to grow and explore and see where it takes you. By allowing its possibilities to inspire you, it can take you on a journey if you trust it. Hopefully you now have even more ideas than the ones I have suggested here, and you are excited about the notion that the tiniest of changes still works toward the greater good.

Start making this world a better place slowly, even if it's just stitch by stitch by stitch. Each of your actions causes a ripple effect, just as each move of your hand around the needle causes a stitch—they create something that wasn't there before, sending creativity, hope, and light out into the world.

abbreviations and terms

Beg = Beginning
CC = Contrasting color
Ch = Chain
Circ = Circular
CO = Cast on
Cont = Continue
DC = Double crochet
Dec = Decrease
Dpn(s) = Double pointed needle(s)
Inc = Increase
Jogless jog = When changing colors at the beginning of a round, lift the right side of the stitch below onto the left needle and knit it together with the stitch.
K = knit
K2tog = knit two stitches together
Kitchener stitch = Insert yarn needle into first st on front needle as if to purl and pull yarn through leaving st on needle. Insert yarn into first st on back needle as if to knit, pull yarn through and leave st on needle. *Insert yarn into first st on front needle as if to knit, pull yarn through, remove st from needle. Insert yarn needle through next st on front needle as if to purl, pull yarn through, leave st on needle. Insert yarn through 1st st on back needle as if to purl, pull yarn through, remove st from needle. Insert yarn needle through next st on back needle as if to knit, pull yarn through, leave st on needle. Repeat from * until 1 st remains on each needle. Cut yarn and pass through st on front needle as to knit, and remove st from needle. Pass through st on back needle as to purl, and remove st from needle.
M = Place marker
M1 = Make 1 stitch by picking up horizontal strand before next st and knitting into back of it.
MC = Main color
P = Purl
P2tog = Purl 2 stitches together
pat = Pattern
Rem = Remain
Rep = Repeat
Rnd(s) = Round(s)
RS = Right side
Sc = Single crochet
Sl st = Slip stitch
Ssk = Sl 2 sts, one at a time as to knit; insert left-hand needle into fronts of both sts from left to right and knit sts together in this position.
St(s) = Stitch(es)
St st = Stockinette Stitch
Tog = Together
WS = Wrong side
Yo = Yarn over

bibliography

Agosin, Marjorie, and Cola Franzen, trans. *Scraps of Life: Chilean Arpilleras.* Trenton, N.J.: Red Sea Press, 1987.

Beal, Susan. *Bead Simple: Essential Techniques for Making Jewelry Just the Way You Want It.* Newtown, Conn.: Taunton Press, 2008.

Beal, Susan, Torie Nguyen, Rachel O'Rourke, and Cathy Pitters. *Super Crafty: Over 75 Amazing How-To Projects!* Seattle: Sasquatch Books, 2005.

Chödrön, Pema. *The Places That Scare You.* Boston: Shambhala Publications, 2002.

Dagen Bloom, Naomi. "History of the Condom Amulet Project." *Knit a Condom Amulet.* www.knitacondomamulet.com/history.html

Goldberg, Carey. "The Power of Om." *The Boston Globe,* November 21, 2005.

Gordon, Debra. "Virtual Reality Pain Distraction." *American Pain Society Bulletin* 15, no. 2 (2005). www.ampainsoc.org/pub/bulletin/spro5/inno1.htm

Levine, Faythe and Cortney Heimerl. *Handmade Nation: The Rise of DIY, Art, Craft, and Design.* New York: Princeton Architectural Press, 2008.

Macdonald, Anne. *No Idle Hands: The Social History of American Knitting.* New York: Ballantine Books, 1988.

Manning, Tara Jon. *Mindful Knitting: Inviting Contemplative Practice to the Craft.* Boston: Tuttle Publishing, 2004.

Pooley, Sue. "Our Family Heritage: A Conversation Between Two Sisters." In *Women and Craft,* edited by G. Elinor, S. Richardson, S. Scott, A. Thomas, and K. Walker. London: Virago, 1987.

Scott, Sue. "Countless Hours: Grandmother's Crochet." In *Women and Craft,* edited by G. Elinor, S. Richardson, S. Scott, A. Thomas, and K. Walker. London: Virago, 1987.

Stoller, Debbie. *Stitch 'n Bitch: The Knitter's Handbook.* New York: Workman Publishing Company, 2004.

U.S. Department of Labor, Bureau of Labor Statistics. "Changes in Women's Labor Force Participation in the 20th Century." *MLR: The Editor's Desk* (February 16, 2000). www.bls.gov/opub/ted/2000/feb/wk3/arto3.htm

We Make Money Not Art. "Interview with Otto von Busch." www.we-make-money-not-art.com/archives/009391.php

Zimmerman, Elizabeth. *Knitting without Tears.* New York: Fireside, 1971.

further resources

Charities and Nonprofits

Afghans for Afghans Project:
Afghansforafghans.org
American Red Cross: Redcross.org
Fine Cell Work: Finecellwork.co.uk
Passage Quilts: Passagequilts.com
Penguin Jumpers Project:
tct.org.au/jumper.htm
Stitch for Senate: Stitchforsenate.us
Subversive Knitting:
subversiveknitting.com
WaterAid: Wateraid.org.uk

Crafty People and Groups

Bryant Holsenbeck: Bryantholsenbeck.com
Cast Off Knitting Club: Castoff.info
Church of Craft: Churchofcraft.org
Craftster: Craftster.org
CraftyPod: Craftypod.com
DIY Alert: DIYAlert.com
Get Crafty: Getcrafty.com
Handmade Nation:
handmadenationmovie.com
Knitta: Knittaplease.com
Knitting History:
Knittinghistory.typepad.com
Knitting SOS: Knittingsos.co.uk
microRevolt: Microrevolt.org
The Missability Radio Show: Missability.com
Obsessive Consumption:
Obsessiveconsumption.com
Radical Cross Stitch: Radicalcrossstitch.com
Revolutionary Knitting Circle:
Knitting.activist.ca
Revolutionary Knitting Front:
Knittingfront.org
>Self_Passage<: Selfpassage.org

Sheep to Shawl: Sheeptoshawl.com
Show Me Your Titles:
Showmeyourtitles.blogspot.com
Stitchlinks: Stitchlinks.com
SuperNaturale: Supernaturale.com
The Switchboards: Theswitchboards.com
Tinkering Times: tinkeringtimes.typepad.com
Tiny Choices: Tinychoices.com
We Make Money Not Art:
We-make-money-not-art.com
Wendy Tremayne: Gaiatreehouse.com
West Coast Crafty: Westcoastcrafty.com
Why Waldorf Works:
Whywaldorfworks.org

Craft Fairs

Art vs. Craft Indie Market: Artvscraft.com
The Bazaar Bizarre: bazaarbizarre.org
DIY Trunk Show: Diytrunkshow.com
The Renegade Craft Fair:
Renegadecraft.com

Shops

Bossa Nova Baby: Bossanovababy.com
Cinnamon Cooper: Poise.cc
Crafty Scientist: Craftyscientist.com
Dear Birthday: dearbirthday.com
Etsy: Etsy.com
I Knit: Iknit.org.uk
Medium Reality: Mediumreality.com
Paper Boat Boutique:
Paperboatboutique.com
Sweet Candy Distro:
eyecandyzine.com
True Stitches: Truestitches.com
Zecca: zecca.net

about the pattern contributors

KATIE AABERG brings fastidious craftsmanship and complex design theory together in her works, which include a range of media: metal arts, bookmaking, comics and zines, felt appliqué, toy design, photography, fiber art, video, and painting. She lives in Eugene, Oregon with her husband and two sons. You can see more of her work at goblinko.com. The Oatlion will be donated to the Womenspace emergency shelter in Eugene. Learn more about Womenspace at enddomesticviolence.com.

LI BOESEN worked in the field of nonprofit management for over twenty-five years, and appreciates the pairing of knitting with charitable efforts. She lives with her family in Vancouver, British Columbia. One of her scarves will be donated to A Place to Call Home Housing Society, a nonprofit set up to address the need for affordable housing in Vancouver.

JANICE BYE worked for more than ten years in the computer business. She retired to stay home with her children, and picked up knitting needles to have something to do while spending many hours in the playground with her three sons. Janice has taught many knitting classes at the Granite State Knit-in, and also at some local shops and knitting guilds. Her socks will be donated to Friends of Boston Homeless. Learn more about them at fobh.com.

NAOMI JOHNSTONE works for Tatty Devine in London. When not traveling around the world, she can be found creating fabulous things while watching *Murder, She Wrote* reruns and drinking tea. Her knitted dog bed was made with her Border terrier, Ludo, in mind and will be donated to the Battersea Dogs Home in London. Learn more about the Battersea Dogs Home at dogshome.org.

ANEETA PATEL is an artist and knitting teacher based in London. She started Knitting SOS in 2005 for knitters in need of emergency help. Her book *Knitty Gritty* will be out in 2008, published by A&C Black. You can learn more about Aneeta at KnittingSOS.co.uk. One of her large cushions will be donated to a local assisted living facility.

FAWN PEA is an environmental activist by day, and a knitter all the time. She lives, hikes, and grows vegetables in North Carolina with her partner and their big, hairy cat. You can find more of her designs at fpea.blogspot.com. One of her mossy jackets will be donated to the Children's Home Society of North Carolina. Learn more about the Children's Home Society at chsnc.org.

LINDA PERMANN is a freelance writer and craft designer. She loves to knit, crochet, sew, and bake. You can learn more about Linda at lindamade.com. One of her Scraps and Stripes hats will be donated to Hats for the Homeless. Learn more about Hats for the Homeless at hats4thehomeless.org.

JUDITH SHANGOLD started designing knitwear in 1976 when she owned a yarn shop in Brooklyn, New York. She was the founder of A Bear in Sheep's Clothing, a fund-raising project that raised money for charitable causes in the 1990s by selling bears dressed in sweaters donated by knitters from around the country. Currently she develops new patterns for her pattern line, Designs by Judith. See more of Judith's work at judithshangold.com. The proceeds from the sales of Judith's pattern will go to Heifer International (heifer international.org).

KELLY WOOTEN is a women's history librarian from North Carolina who has been knitting for about four years. Her basket-weave blanket will be donated to Project Linus. Learn more about Project Linus at projectlinus.org.